LOST IN THE CHAOS
*Immanence, Despair, Hope*

R. J. SNELL

# Lost in the Chaos

*Immanence, Despair, Hope*

Angelico Press

For information, address:
Angelico Press
169 Monitor St.
Brooklyn, NY 11222
info@angelicopress.com

ISBN 978-1-62138-955-2 (pbk)
ISBN 978-1-62138-957-6 (cloth)
ISBN 978-1-62138-958-3 (ebook)

Cover Design: Michael Schrauzer

*For the BC boys, old friends*

# CONTENTS

# Preface

IN 1983 Walker Percy released *Lost in the Cosmos: The Last Self-Help Book*.[1] It's difficult to categorize, in part because it satirizes the self-help genre while critiquing Carl Sagan's famous *Cosmos*, explores Percy's semiotic theory of the self, posits discomfiting thought experiments, and ends with the collapse of civilization. *Lost in the Cosmos* is very strange.[2] Beyond the genre and the satire, the text is odd in questioning the meaning and mystery of the self—who are we, why are we here, how do we learn who we are? Since humans are always problems to themselves, there is a certain timelessness to these queries, but in the current intellectual mood they feel a bit quaint. Many now obsess over politics and power; the inner depths of psychology dissolve into neuroscience; the personal self vanishes into impersonal structures of race, sex, gender, or class. Older, existential questions about the purpose of human life are notably absent in many universities, for instance, replaced with the assumptions of reductionism and the immanentized universe.

If we are merely "star stuff," as claimed by Sagan, a combination of hardware and software better explained by chemistry than theology, and if our values and mores are simply cultural memes, then many of Percy's questions, the same questions asked by earlier philosophers and theolo-

---

[1] Walker Percy, *Lost in the Cosmos: The Last Self-Help Book* (New York: Picador, 1983).

[2] A small section of this appeared in "Lost in the Chaos: The Danger of Total Politics," *Public Discourse* (August 18, 2021).

1

gians, appear mildly ridiculous. *Lost in the Cosmos* belongs to an older world, one in which *cosmos* was a meaningful term, even if drawing its final breaths. For the Stoics, *kosmos* indicated the beauty and harmony of the world, including its knowability by reason. As cosmos, the universe functioned like an organism, its systems and operations contributing to the ordered whole. Against *cosmos* lurks its opposite, *chaos*, a lack of order, wildness. In the cosmology of Hesiod, chaos existed first and divine beings were born from it. In cosmos, however, the inner principle of all things was *logos*, rationality, a divine, perfect order.

For moderns, as stipulated by Luc Ferry, the idea of cosmos "gives us a sense of how remote this way of thinking is from our own. If anyone claimed today that the world . . . possesses a soul and is endowed with reason—he would be considered crazy."[3] Postmodernism and its progenitors critiqued and deconstructed any and every claim of order, harmony, or rationality as nothing more than projections of power and force. Chaos reigns, and reason itself is nothing more than a chaotic attempt to enforce a fictitious and utterly arbitrary "order" on the flux. According to Nietzsche, cosmos is a "supreme untruth," and removing explicit reference to God or logos while smuggling similar assumptions into human rationality refuses to admit the actual world order—force. As it turns out, the ancients, Christians, and Enlightenment thinkers share a commit-

---

[3] Luc Ferry, *A Brief History of Thought: A Philosophical Guide to Living*, trans. Theo Cuffe (New York: Harper Perennial, 2011), 17–24, 143–97. To reduce the distraction of citations, I cite page ranges; unless noted, and until the next footnote, all subsequent quotations are from that range.

ment to order and to reason, but thorough honesty sees things more starkly: war is the father of all.

In Ferry's telling, while Enlightenment figures such as Descartes and Kant remained committed to the idea of rationality, their suspicion and scorn for the medievals created a critical spirit that could not be contained once infused into the Western mind: "Like the sorcerer's apprentice who unleashed forces which soon escape his control, Descartes and the Enlightenment philosophers unleashed a critical spirit which, once in motion, could not be stopped, somewhat like an acid that continues to eat into the materials with which it comes in contact. . . ." The acid of critique rampaged unabated, eventually dissolving the confidence and vitality of modern rationalism itself, now considered an idol constructed by men.

The contemporary mind, then, is not, as Percy thought, lost in the cosmos, not adrift in an ordered world; instead, our moment is lost in chaos. Interestingly, however, this is not experienced by many contemporaries as especially troubling. The anguish of Ivan and Alyosha in *The Brothers Karamazov* about whether God exists, the pugnacity of Camus against false Christians, the Sartrean anxiety about God's absence—all this seems outdated and *passé*. The dread, angst, anxiety, even horror of God's non-existence appears childish or hopelessly quaint. Why? How could the loss of God arouse so little reaction?

A flattened universe goes hand-in-hand with flattened humans. Postmodern people, unlike earlier non-believers, do not experience the loss of God "as a trauma, an affront, a source of anguish," since they don't "experience it at all."[4] No tragedy to this loss since it was never felt as a loss, and even if the "death of God involves the death of Man," this, too, is not experienced, since the human is thought so flat as not to possess the "space" in which either God or a self could reside. Not only the image of God has disappeared, but also those inner depths where a self might hide. Generations raised without God have culture, psychology, literature, and morality stuck in the shallows and view "depth and interiority," and the self linked to such depths, as belonging "to a clapped-out metaphysics" so alien it isn't even knowingly rejected.

All this is despair. A world of sheer and utter immanence is a world without hope, although various false and utterly disappointing versions of "hope" emerge as substitutes for the real thing. This book explores radical immanence, the resulting despair, false and flailing attempts to provide hope, and hope in its genuine meaning. Ours is a hopeless age, but it doesn't follow that hope is unavailable. If you'd like to find hope, I might be able to point the way. Before that, though, I tell a troubled story, first of malaise and despair, then of false and feverish attempts to construct hope, but, in the end, after we've looked despair full in the face, we turn to a true—a very true—account of hope. Hope is on the far side of despair. Honest despair is a halfway house for hope.

In the first three chapters, I explore radical immanence, the loss of value, and the failure of hope—three malaises of modernity. In chapters 4–6, false versions of hope are examined, namely, humanitarianism (of a certain sort), political rationalism, and false attempts to re-enchant the world—three temptations, idylls, trying to escape malaise. In the final chapters, I offer paths for recovering hope,

---

[4] Terry Eagleton, *Culture and the Death of God* (New Haven, CT: Yale University Press, 2014), 185–87.

including a dynamic ontology, a supple cognitional theory, and the virtue of hope. Three malaises, three idylls, three avenues of hope.

I have benefited from presenting these ideas to several audiences. With that in mind, I owe much to participants of First Principles, a summer seminar hosted by the Witherspoon Institute, as well as its teachers David Corey, Anna Moreland, and Karen Taliaferro. Also to my dear friend Rabbi Mark Gottlieb, and the Tikvah Scholars Program, where he and I have co-taught The Nature of Reason in Western and Jewish Thought. I've learned much from Mark, not only as a scholar and teacher but as a man of kindness and humanity. Thanks are happily given to my colleagues and friends at the Witherspoon Institute, especially Luis Tellez, Kelly Hanlon, and Robert P. George. I'm delighted to dedicate a book to Athan, Graham, and Harrison, with whom I have read and argued for years, surely more to my benefit than theirs. Always, to that little outpost of joy which is my family, particularly Amy, who taught me the primacy of the person better than any theories. She's light when I'm unable to see.

With gratitude I acknowledge *Public Discourse: The Journal of the Witherspoon Institute*, of which I am editor-in-chief; its wonderful group of contributing editors; and Elayne Allen, our most recent managing editor, for good counsel and friendship, and for permission to use material previously appearing there, although revised and reconfigured for this book, and appearing mostly in chapter 5:

"Lost in the Chaos: The Danger of Total Politics," *Public Discourse* (August 18, 2021).

"Don't Panic," *Public Discourse* (August 20, 2022).

"How Should Conservatives Respond to Revolution?" *Public Discourse* (April 4, 2023).

"The Truth of Sensible Politics," *Public Discourse* (May 15, 2023).

# PART I

## Losing Our Religion

# 1

## *Inanis et Vacua*

ENGLISH TRANSLATIONS have turned the novelist Elena Ferrante, long known and praised in Italy, into an international sensation. The so-called Neapolitan novels have received much attention as well as a television adaptation, and several of the shorter novels have film adaptations planned or already released. The mystique surrounding the author adds to the phenomenon as well. Elena Ferrante is a pen name prompting much speculation about the identity of the author. Is it a woman, a man, a husband-and-wife team? I do not praise the despair of these novels, nor do I share it, but their brutality captures the despair felt by many people. We cannot offer hope if we do not adequately understand our moment.

Nonetheless, this first chapter is full of desperate, unsettling despair, drawing on the fiction of Ferrante to exemplify it. As I'll suggest and explain in subsequent chapters, I don't take Ferrante to explore merely her own emotional turmoil or personal attitudes, but, rather, to exemplify a widespread, almost ubiquitous horror at the conditions of life. She's brutal, yes, but reveals a common experience. I'm glad if my readers have normal, happy lives, and they might read this chapter as odd and overstated, and yet I do suggest the despair and hopelessness of Ferrante's characters are broadly true of contemporary society. Furthermore, since the conditions of modernity, explored in chapters 2–3, contribute to, and in some ways logically lead to, the heart-wrenching unhappiness of real people, it is charitable to look despair full in the face so as to recognize the suffering of many of our neighbors and friends. Even more, if we look at despair clearly, without sentiment or nostalgia, we can better understand the attraction, the somewhat desperate appeal, of false versions of hope—idylls—examined in chapters 4–6. Honesty, however blunt, sets up the path to recovering hope in chapters 7–9.

The book ends in hope; indeed, it ends with the greatest hope imaginable, the willing acceptance of divine life exemplified by the Virgin Mary. First, though, radical immanence and its attendant despair, exemplified by disgust and loathing at pregnancy and motherhood in Ferrante's fiction. An unhappy, anti-Marian beginning to our story, which will, nevertheless, end in Marian hope.

The novels explore the experience of women, generally women subjected to mistreatment by men. Ferocity and rage radiate from the texts, sometimes shockingly. Women are beaten, threatened, and reviled, often responding in kind. In *The Lost Daughter*, for instance, Leda walks to her car after a day at the beach before hearing footsteps and receiving "a violent blow" as if "with a billiard ball."[1] The novel ends with her losing consciousness in a car accident after being stabbed in the abdomen with a hat pin, accompanied with "hissing insults in dialect, terrible as the ones

---

[1] Elena Ferrante, *The Lost Daughter*, trans. Ann Goldstein (New York: Europa, 2008).

my grandmother, my mother used to utter." Leda has inflicted harm on herself, stealing a young child's doll, a beloved plaything and "baby," to the immense distress of the girl and her family. Leda recoils from the doll with disgust, just as she rejected her own daughters when infants, placing the doll "in a painful position, arms spread, legs apart, lying on her back, her head half buried in the sand. Her nose could be seen, an eye, half her skull." Later, examining the doll in her apartment, she realizes the doll is leaking a dark liquid that stains her skirt, as Leda, revolted, "imagined a stomach filth, a stale stagnant liquid mixed with sand." Leda is horrified at pregnancy, her own and others, describing the changes made to her body as "a round life that is yours . . . pushes elsewhere, draws away from you although it inhabits your belly, joyful and weighty, felt as a greedy impulse and yet repellent, like an insect's poison injected into a vein." Such new life is to be "expelled."

Leda, like many women in Ferrante's novels, is divorced, and has alienated her children, who join their father overseas to be free of her desire to expel their "alien closeness." Leda is similar to Olga, the protagonist of *The Days of Abandonment*, which begins with Olga's husband blandly announcing as they cleared dishes that he was leaving her, although he does so with composure, reproaching no one.[2] Mario "closed the front door carefully behind him" and was gone, not even saying farewell to the children. At first he attempts a semblance of routine, returning to their apartment to play with their two children and the dog, but Olga's "anguish and rage was growing" within her, terrified

---

[2] Elena Ferrante, *The Days of Abandonment*, trans. Ann Goldstein (New York: Europa, 2005).

she would become like a woman she knew from her own childhood, also abandoned by her husband, an object of scorn and embarrassment. That woman lost everything, "even her name," and became known simply as "the *poverella*, that poor woman," who shriveled and shambled about the neighborhood.

Although Olga attempts "affectionate thoughtfulness" to Mario, she's convinced he is attempting to disgust her, to make her push him away, to say, "get out, you make me sick, I can't stand you anymore." He wants her to conclude the marriage is over, to renounce him, to avoid responsibility for the divorce.

And then, it happens. In a fit of distraction, she cuts herself while cooking and drops a wine bottle, sending shards of glass throughout the room, including into the sauce. That night, she serves him dinner, angrily demanding to know if he has found another woman, which he admits before biting into the meal:

> He had begun to chew in his usual methodical way, but suddenly something cracked in his mouth. He stopped chewing, his fork fell on his plate, he groaned. Now he was spitting what was in his mouth into the palm of his hand, pasta and sauce and blood, it was really blood, red blood. . . . [His] eyes wide, he wiped off his hand with the napkin, stuck his fingers in his mouth, and pulled out of his palate a splinter of glass.

With this, all pretense gone, he shrieks at her, smashes the chair repeatedly on the floor, slams the door, and departs for his new lover.

Olga is abandoned, in free fall. She cannot calm herself,

cannot believe it possible that Mario has left. How had he "become uninterested in my life, like a plant watered for years that is abruptly allowed to die of drought," no longer worth attending? She feels "over every inch of my body the scratches of sexual abandonment." In short order, she rejects all who attempt to help her, loses the habit of careful dress and makeup, and becomes sarcastic, mocking, and obscene in her speech. She abandons herself to pornography, wondering if Mario's new woman performs such acts, and lives "like a sleepwalker." Seeing Mario in the street, she erupts in a fit of obscenity and vileness, in front of the children. Abandoned by a man, she is unloved and does not love, viewing her own children as loathsome and repellent. They have consumed her, she feels, first Mario and then the children, and she is like "a lump of food that my children chewed without stopping; a cud made of a living material that continually amalgamated and softened its living substance to allow two greedy bloodsuckers to nourish themselves." She is nothing, has become nothing, and will never return.

In a misguided and desperate plan to overcome her abandonment, she attempts an affair with a neighbor, Carrano. Rather than giving her a sense of vitality and desirability to counter her husband's much younger lover, the episode ends only in humiliation, rejection, and self-loathing, prompting the greatest "ordeal" of her abandonment.

The morning after the failed attempt at an affair, she awakens in a state of profound disorientation, suffering vertigo of both space and time, confusing grammatical tenses. She does not recognize her bedroom, and is sleeping sideways in the bed, so doesn't see, as usual, the closet but a wall without definition or focal point. Her feet "looked out on a void" with "no explanation." Her bedroom is foreign to her, with none of the usual constants allowing a fixed position.

Her young daughter, Ilaria, complains that her brother, Gianni, was ill in the night, throwing up on Ilaria's bed and suffering a dangerously high fever. As she cleans the mess, Olga is sickened less by vomit than by motherhood's effects on her body, softening and weighing her as it has done. She expects "a moment that never arrived, the moment when I would be again as I had been before my pregnancies, young, slender, energetic, shamelessly certain I could make of myself a memorable person." During this episode, she fixates on her perceived loss of beauty, a loss inevitable, she thinks, for all women, turning all into the *poverella*.

Again Gianni is sick; again she cleans him, sinking into madness. She cannot read the thermometer, struggles to maintain focus, to pay attention, certain that "after months of tension I had arrived at the edge of some precipice and now I was falling, as in a dream, slowly. . . ." She threatens to hit the children, slaps herself instead, and begins to bleed. Pain keeps her in reality, and she bites herself, places a binder clip on her skin, asks her daughter to prod her with a papercutter. She needs a tranquilizer, she concludes, and worries less about her son and more that she is losing herself. Desperately she runs a bath to clean up, allowing the tub to overflow with cold water while doing her makeup, locked in the bathroom. Later she will lock the children in their room.

In the middle of this madness, an awful odor confronts her, not her son's vomit but the bloody stool, drool, and vomit of the dog, perhaps poisoned by Carrano, who had threatened to do so, or by insecticide she used for ants without disposing of the aerosol can. These very ants now crawl on the dying dog, swarming his body and its effluence. To Olga's disgust, the dog squirms into his master's study—the husband who has abandoned her—as if looking for comfort from Mario. Gianni requests she "call Daddy." Never mind that he's useless, a deadbeat father, or that she is here, with Gianni in his need. He repeats, "but call Daddy." Daddy, the one "who knew what to do, had left. We had to manage by ourselves."

Daddy would have acted, would have called for help, so Olga eventually gathers herself into enough coherence to call the vet and doctor. The telephone, however, does not work, emitting only a faint hissing sound of static—she has neglected to pay the bill, as recounted much earlier in the book when she threatens violence against the telephone workers. Now, only silence: "I pretended and I avoided responsibility for the children, the dog, with the cold pantomime of one who knows and does." Still, nothing more than an odd whistling sound from the receiver. The cell phone, too, is broken. Broken by her, split into halves which she now fumbles to reassemble and rubber-band together, to no avail.

She has no connection. No connection to the world outside of herself and her abandonment. She has become the *poverella*, hallucinating that sad, impoverished woman in the mirror, taking advice from a woman dead for decades, now more capable and knowing than Olga. The *poverella* reminds Olga about the dying dog and ill son. She must act. Olga gets up and makes for the door, but "slowed down immediately," knowing her vision of being "decisive," one who will "remedy things," is a fancy. She decelerates, addressing herself in the third person, as a non-agent:

"Olga has a terror of the frenzy of doing, she fears that the need for a prompt reaction . . . will migrate into her brain." She resets the "bite" of the paper clip to "get me to abandon that third person" and return to herself, who knows who she is, and controls what she does.

Olga decides to ask her neighbor for help—Carrano, the cause of her humiliation the previous night. He alone remains in the apartment building during the holiday season, all others being on vacation. He alone can help her, and she determines to ask, as a last resort, a final hope. The key in the door won't turn, however. It is jammed, immoveable. Some months before, Olga, worried Mario was sneaking into the apartment to remove her things, had hired workmen to install new locks and reinforce the door. Now the key will not turn, nor can she extract it from the lock: "it wouldn't come out, it remained in the key-hole as if metal had fused to metal. . . . I was consumed by desperation." She gathers tools, but the screwdrivers are too big, too small; the door too strong to pry off its hinges, too solid to knock apart. She is trapped.

Just then, Ilaria appears, garishly costumed in a wig and Olga's shoes, dress, and makeup: "her face was a painted mask . . . she looked to me like an old dwarf." Olga finds her loathsome and cannot disguise it, to which Ilaria says, "we're identical." Olga responds viciously, dragging Ilaria harshly down the hall to the tub full of freezing cold water, holding her by the head and immersing her while savagely washing her face, almost drowning her.

Olga orders Ilaria to bang on the floor with a hammer, hoping to attract Carrano's attention, while Olga again reverts to the third person, disassociating, staring at two images of herself in panels of a mirror showing her as ugly, incapable, and lacking self-possession. She is a pastiche constructed by the desires of Mario, and she "recognized the features of the *poverella*" who had "been huddling in me for years." She eventually remembers the dog and Gianni, who cries, "I called you and you didn't come." Ants swarm the dog; the phones provide no connection; the apartment block is empty; the door immoveable. She is trapped in this room with its disgusting stench of death, vomit, and stool. Trying the phone, she "hoped for a sort of magic. . . . Nothing, nothing, nothing."

Eventually, the dog dies, with "an intense pain in his body," a gnashing of teeth and a final bark. Olga bursts out in tears, "crying in an uncontrollable lament, utterly unlike any other crying of those days, those months." Suddenly, without warning, the doorbell rings, prompting this response from Ilaria: "'Daddy,' murmured Ilaria, full of hope."

It is not her father. Her hope is for nought.

I can think of no fiction better conveying the self-imposed reality of the modern person. Three elements stand out, which I'll briefly summarize here and explore in the chapters to follow, namely, radical immanence, the absence of value, and the failure of hope.

God transcends the physical universe as its creator and sustainer. The universe cannot create itself, since nothing can be the cause of its own existence, and orthodox Christianity rightly holds that God cannot be another entity within the universe of entities. Too frequently, people misunderstand the arguments for God's existence and imagine God as the first being in a chain of beings visualized as a horizontal line on a chalkboard, with the right side of the line representing the universe as it now is and the far-left stopping point indicating God. This is mistaken; it would reduce God to another entity in the line of entities, and He would be part (albeit first) of the same series we are attempting to explain. That doesn't work. It would turn God into the biggest, most powerful, smartest thing of them all, but still another thing among things, an immanentized deity, an Olympian—more than merely human, but a difference of degree rather than kind, more superhuman than divine.

Consequently, the genuinely Christian account doesn't posit God as merely first but as *beyond*, yonder, as transcending the universe. God is not first on the timeline so much as entirely outside the timeline, not a member of the set. In the beginning, Genesis states, the earth was "void and empty, and darkness was upon the face of the deep" (1.2). "Void and empty" translates the Hebrew *tohu wa bohu*, emptiness and waste. The Vulgate says *inanis et vacua*, an emptiness, void of anything, a vacuum. This suggests the idea of creation *ex nihilo*; there is nothing (other than God) and then something: light, waters, land, lights, fowl and fish, plants and animals, including the human animal. God, full act and necessary being, cannot be part of the nothingness, cannot partake of *inanis et vacua*, but is *beyond*. God is transcendent.

For Olga there is no beyond. She is trapped in her apartment. No landline, no cell phone, no window or door to exit. She is confined within, with "nothing, nothing, nothing" beyond. And within this room, within this life? Illness, confusion, stench, and death. It couldn't be more clear: there once was a Daddy who could have acted and helped

—the age of belief in the Father, in God—but Daddy has left. Moderns consider themselves alone in this universe, with no God and no advent of help. What remains is that illness which is life, already in the inexorable trajectory toward death—birth is the beginning of a slow death. Olga's fretting about beauty's loss has nothing on Gerard Manley Hopkins's statement of our fate: "ruck and wrinkle, drooping, dying, death's worst, winding/sheets, tombs and worms and tumbling to decay." We are all the *poverella. Inanis et vacua.*

If there is no transcendent God, the void and nothing remain. No accident that Olga awakens confused, feet hanging into the void, without orientation to time and space. Rational agency requires actions have a point, directed to a goal, or purpose. We distinguish a simple behavior—like respiration—from a voluntary action in that action has the structure of a proposal. Some means or instrument, $x$, is chosen to bring about some state of affairs, $y$, in order that some good, $z$, can be obtained or enacted. It makes no sense to choose $x$ without $y$ or $z$ as part of the proposal. If I am digging a hole in my front yard and a neighbor asks what I'm doing, it would be unintelligible if I responded, "digging a hole, of course." He knows that already; he is not perplexed by the movement of shovel into soil. Rather, he's asking *why* I'm digging, and should I have no answer to *why*, then I'm doing something bizarre. If I dig *in order to* plant a tree *so as to* provide shade for a patio, it all makes sense. My action is coherent.

But maybe that's too hasty. As Aristotle noted in the *Nicomachean Ethics*, my proposal's mere structure is incomplete without an intrinsically purposive end, a reason sufficient to explain why I'm acting. For instance, planting a tree for shade isn't really coherent unless we assume that someone will sit in that shade in order to converse with friends, eat a meal with family, read a book, or watch the birds. A chair in the shade means nothing in itself, and engaging in labor to bring about a shaded chair is pointless inane and vacuous, *inanis et vacua* unless in service of intrinsic goods like friendship, play, or knowledge. As Aristotle articulates, every action seeks some good, but not all goods are intrinsically choice-worthy: "we do not choose everything because of something else—for if we do, it will go on without limit, so that desire will prove to be empty and futile."[3]

Aristotle explains the structure of intelligibility, but does not demonstrate that things are actually intelligible. *If* actions are intelligible rather than futile, they seek something intrinsically worth choosing. What if there isn't anything worth choosing? What if actions are futile, pointless, and void? Isn't that a real possibility?

Olga confronts this very issue. Consider her horror at discovering Ilaria dressed in her mother's clothes—"we're identical." At this, Olga drags Ilaria to wash, tearing off wig and clothing in the process. "Like me . . . would be horrible." Olga sees her life as pointless. She is abandoned; her husband consumed her body and identity, just as the children, like vampires, emptied her of meaning. She is emptiness, the *poverella*, one whose identity is poor, vacant, evacuated. Olga, in her own eyes, is as nothing, and none of her actions do, will, or could mean anything.

Her despair is heightened by aging. No longer sexually

---

[3] Aristotle, *Nicomachean Ethics*, trans. Terence Irwin (Indianapolis: Hackett Publishing, 1999), I.2, 1094a20–22.

attractive, she cannot arouse the interest of others, and the very point of sexuality—husband and children—disgust her and leave her empty. That her daughter is identical to her is not a source of pride or joy but horror. What she had "feared most" since childhood was "to grow up and become like the *poverella*," and Ilaria "was only returning to me my true image. . . . I was no longer I." Such, Olga suggests, is the fate of all women, recalling the *poverella*'s lament that she was left with "the odor of motherhood" and "ruined" by pregnancy, a sentiment Olga's own mother had "repeated," "gravely agreeing." Generation after generation, motherhood ruined women, taking their youth and life but leaving them with nothing, all to be repeated by their daughters and granddaughters. The existence of children and grandchildren is not considered a good in itself; human existence is not worthwhile, on this account.

No action has purpose, and in the end death erases all. Without a transcendent vantage point from which to view our actions, they lack sufficient ground. Even if goods could be described as intrinsically worthwhile, what difference does it make, given the contingency and transience of those goods? All is dust, in the end, and no good depending on our choice or act survives; even were that to happen, we will not survive to know. Given this perspective, is it any surprise that the West faces demographic collapse? The United States is below replacement births, with the lowest level of marriage in recorded history and lowest birth rates outside times of crisis and war. A surprising number of the young ponder whether it is moral to have children and some, just in their teens, undergo voluntary sterilization. Others simply "check out," or, as it is called in Japan, suffer from *hikikomori* (social withdrawal), especially young men,

21

who withdraw into basements and the online world. "What is the point?"

We can find an activity pointless without falling into despair, after all. Sometimes work is mere drudgery, nothing more than busy work. Still, we tend to put up with drudgery when it has instrumental value. We endure a particularly unpleasant task to keep a job or earn a credential, for example, but how are we to understand merely instrumental activity—which we would not choose for its own sake—if the state of affairs brought about by that toil is itself thought pointless? I'll exercise, which I dislike, for the sake of health, which I rather enjoy, but why would I diet if it made no difference to my health, or, worse, if dieting contributed to my ill health? In the absence of a higher good, or if no goods are worthwhile in themselves, why bother?

Not only is the good evacuated of purpose, but suffering even more so. Pain is endured, sometimes even elevated or redeemed, when it serves a purpose. The pain of a mother in labor is intense, even harrowing, but harrowing in another sense of the term as well, as in the "harrowing of hell," when Christ's descent released hell's captives. The agony of a beloved wife is terrible, and yet no husband can ever forget his wife's cry of joy—what wonder!—when a newly delivered child is placed on her breast. She reaches out, eager to receive this person into her embrace, and would endure it all again for this son, this daughter.

Olga, on the other hand, suspects her son is sexually attracted to her husband's new lover. Not only is she sexually abandoned by her husband, but the fruit of their relationship—a child—will lust for and desire the cause of her rejection, or so she assumes. And that her daughter is like her—will become her—is horrifying. She experienced childbirth and nursing as being used, consumed, and destroyed. This revulsion is even more apparent in Leda in *The Lost Daughter*, whose children have abandoned her, following their father to escape her hectoring. Encountering the doll she has stolen fills her with disgust. Its belly, awash in silt and sea water, horrifies her, indicating the filth of pregnancy, like an insect's poison, that is not delivered—or harrowed—but "expelled."

We can be maudlin and sentimental about children, to be sure, and yet it remains true that to generate and welcome new life is an act of generosity and of hope, an affirmation that life is worthwhile, good enough to give to another. A child is a sign of hope, not merely in the rather boring sense that they might be able to do something to improve the world, but in a far more remarkable sense—we have joined two lives into one in order that another might be, might exist, and we think it good that they now *are*. A mother in labor delivers a child from possible death; delivery is a kind of salvation, and claims that *it is good to be*. That so few now have children, and so few children at that, and, more, that so many children are destroyed in their mother's womb, is the great mark of our society's despair, its perverse judgment that it is *not* good to be, not worth giving life to another. Men provide only an insect's poison, and to gestate is to bring the poisoned into existence. Life itself is poisoned, already a dying, never more than a vale of suffering and tears, *lacrimarum valle*.

If there is a point to life, if there is a point even beyond this life, suffering can be understood as mystery and not simply as a problem, to use the terms of Gabriel Marcel. Problems are to be solved, and the problem disappears in its solution. Not so a mystery, because *we* are caught up into the issue, perhaps even are the issue. Once the test is finished, I relax and move on to the next task or to rest. But I can never move on from myself, for I am a mystery to myself and my attempts to wrestle with myself involve me as my own opponent, and there is no obvious way of putting the challenge to rest. The mystery of suffering is not resolvable, for even if we were able to end all pain from this day forward, the unpalatable fact of past suffering remains a challenge to our vision of the world and God as good. Suffering cannot simply be solved; it must, somehow, be redeemed, incorporated into meaning, into purpose. Suffering can be resolved, ultimately, only if all things, even the shattering and awful, are incorporated or recapitulated into goodness. Without that hope, suffering is pointless, irredeemable, and absurd (Ivan in *The Brothers Karamazov* knew this). In a world of radical immanence, redemption is impossible and there is no hope. In such a case, wisdom, to return to Hopkins, is to "be beginning, be beginning to despair."

Many in our time have taken this advice; many have given in to despair. They are not irrational to do so, lost in the chaos as they are. *Inanis et vacua*. Against this, against *all* of this, we can hope.

# 2

## Disenchanted Immanence

PERHAPS NO ONE explores the history of immanence as
well as Charles Taylor in *A Secular Age*, where he places contemporary experience within the "immanent frame."[1] In
Taylor's account, an important difference between our time
and earlier is what counts as *fullness*, moving from "a condition in which our highest spiritual and moral aspirations
point us inescapably to God . . . [and] make no sense without God, to one in which they can be related to a host of
different sources." A world in which the highest and best of
the human can be fulfilled without God is categorically different than a world where they cannot. Unlike earlier forms
of humanism, "exclusive humanism" precludes any more
than merely human source of meaning. It is not indifferent
or agnostic but actively removes God from its understanding of well-being, flourishing, and human accomplishment.

Taylor rejects the "subtraction thesis" and its claims that
faith was destined to fade when knowledge increased. This
thesis holds that, lacking explanations for ordinary events,
the pre-modern mind attributed causality to gods and spirits, and thus it was easy to believe in God. However, once
"real" explanations—meaning scientific, or naturalistic—

---

[1] Charles Taylor, *A Secular Age* (Cambridge, MA: Belknap Press,
2007). Unless indicated, quotations are from that text.

became available, faith disappeared, since the need for the supernatural was "subtracted" from life. Not so, claims Taylor; it didn't happen that way historically, and Christianity itself tends towards demythologization by rejecting idols and polytheism. Providence allows for natural secondary causes and demands the integrity and functioning of nature, sanctifying the natural world and its processes with the doctrines of creation and incarnation. The supernatural doesn't vanish when nature is esteemed or animism rejected.

Disenchantment certainly occurred, however. Consider a fairly mundane example, one Taylor uses: Candlemas. There was a time when the faithful brought candles to be blessed with the Paschal candle, taking into their ordinary candles something of the "power" of the Paschal candle, turning them into sacramentals. The candles were then *charged*, as it were, the way holy water is charged, more than just ordinary water, infused or participating in some efficacy beyond the power to bathe or to light. In a stormy night, when devils prowled or ghosts haunted, re-lighting the blessed candle not only enkindled light with its power to calm but also presented the power of the Paschal candle itself, a power strong enough to keep devils at bay.

In analogous ways, the chalking of a door, planting or harvesting crops on certain propitious feast days, or parading a relic around a field to prevent locusts reveals an enchanted world. In addition to accepting that things have powers, enchantment views objects and people as *porous*. Power can enter into things, either benevolent or malevolent power. The candle is no longer merely wax, wick, and flame, but a sacramental—the power of the Paschal candle, itself no mere candle, has entered into it, transformed it somehow. The sanctity of the relic enters the one who venerates it; the evil eye or hex actually infects a person; bread appears as bread but *is* something quite different. Things are porous. Power can go into and out of things, into and out of persons, for nothing is perfectly self-contained or impermeable, what Taylor calls "buffered."

We no longer live in an enchanted world. Imaginations may give in to fancy at the bump in the night, but we are quick to say, "it's nothing, only the dog, at worst a burglar." We're slow to conclude a ghost or devil is in the house, and even slower to reach for a holy candle to exorcise the demon. Even religious people who believe in devils and faithfully recite the St Michael prayer might feel a sort of embarrassment. We don't *first* think devils are near, even if we finally conclude so, and the normal and well-adjusted among us hesitate to tell the priest, let alone the neighbors, of their spooky visitors.

Of course, we know people who do think of ghosts and devils first and wind, dogs, or robbers at last resort. They're weird. Odd. Mildly embarrassing if distant acquaintances, mortifying if an in-law. It's difficult to avoid thinking of them as superstitious, even if we believe in the supernatural. Even stranger are the mystery-mongers, those who see the work of angels and demons frequently—*too* frequently. They should know what causes thunder; they're not children, after all. They're like people who attend Renaissance Faires or comic conventions in full regalia as knights or superheroes. The type who take Tolkien a bit too far and learn Elvish or own a "replica" of Gandalf's staff. Such people are role-playing, cosplaying, and they should grow up already. Or, and this is Taylor's point, for modern people it is very easy to take this tone.

At the same time, this dismissive attitude is compatible

with religious belief. Many people believe in God and the Christian claims of incarnation and resurrection while simultaneously rolling their eyes at sacraments, let alone sacramentals, charged objects, and porous reality. Christians who accept the seven sacraments, and thus a sort of porous capacity in the world, are more likely to recommend a visit to the doctor or the therapist than a priest when a lump is discovered or voices heard. It's no longer intuitive and obvious to look to the supernatural to explain what is fully intelligible with a natural account. We are accustomed to a sort of "nothing but-ism" in our lives, as in "that's nothing but a chemical imbalance, and not possession."

Consequently, faith, while certainly not immediately subtracted, is on its back foot in a disenchanted world. It needn't be the starting point or first principle for leading a normal life, nor in leading a *full* life. Fullness is possible, or at least a good many people assert as much, with a hefty bank account, health, good friends, recreation, and technological gadgetry. Believers look over their shoulders to see how other people are doing, and it turns out they seem to be doing just fine—sometimes better—despite (even because) they inhabit a world of exclusive humanism devoid of charge and spirit and supernatural (or preternatural) power. Their world is flattened, obviously, one-dimensional, lacking vertical relation between this world and the world beyond, and yet they seem satisfied, content, and full. And though believers are not so *obviously* embarrassing as the man dressed as Gandalf, we realize it's entirely possible our friends and neighbors view faith as quaint, ridiculous, naïve, or fantastical. All this to say, the conditions of belief have changed; faith is not obvious and easy and assumed, and all know this to be true. Faith is an option among many, and fullness takes many forms, not merely the form of the Christian claim.

Certainly religious belief persists. Taylor does not claim religion inevitably disappears or is likely to do so; rather, the "conditions of belief" change. It's not that moderns are necessarily secular in the sense of not believing in God or not practicing a religion, but the context in which people believe is secular. Everyone knows there are other options, everyone knows there are competing accounts, and everyone knows those competing accounts are not viewed as abnormal in the current milieu. It was perhaps somewhat difficult to be an atheist in thirteenth-century Paris, while it is exceptionally easy in the City of Lights of the twenty-first. Belief persists, but it is not an obvious, self-evident starting point. Faith is optional, needing to defend itself as a live option in ways quite different from previous moments in the West.

As mentioned earlier, a cosmos governed by reason allowed enchantment. A world created by God the Father through the Son by the power of the Holy Spirit is a luminous world, not a rationalistic universe. Things were charged with the grandeur of God, a good "magic" allowing Candlemas and sacramentals and sacraments. A small conceptual change, however, transposes the cosmos into a *universe*, changes *creation* into *nature*, and universe/nature can be denuded, disenchanted. The prevalent understanding of the universe is rationalistic, governed by laws of nature with no room for charged objects, porous selves, or sacraments. Instead of things indicating, containing, or even *being* the glory of God, things became sheerly factical. Matter in motion requires no explanation other than physics and chemistry.

The universe understood as matter in motion fits a picture of what Taylor terms the "buffered self." Things don't have charges rendering us or good or bad, nor are humans permeable. Humans are autonomous individuals, self-enclosed, atomized, like Leibniz's monads with neither windows nor doors to be permeated. The world lost its charged power, and we lost our receptivity to charge; a universe of matter in motion reduces humans to matter in motion, "wet robots" as we are sometimes called.

## The Age of Reform

While the buffered self loses something in disenchantment, it gains something as well: autonomy. If humans cannot be permeated by alien powers then humans are self-directed, independent, and autonomous. As Taylor tells the story, this change allows for the age of Reform, an attempt to promote human development and perfection through human means.

The enchanted age of "magic" is hospitable to, and perhaps even requires, mediation and hierarchy. If an otherwise normal physical object can be charged with force and power not its own, that object can act as a medium through which the actual source and cause of that power is presented or represented. One thing presents another, mediates another, and the object acting as mediator is in some sense more than itself, containing something beyond it. In classical theology, the Eucharist is a clear example of this. What was normal bread and wine is no longer but contains—is!—something else entirely. The appearance of bread persists, but the substance is transposed. Further, it is fitting, or natural, for mediation to entail hierarchy. In hierarchy, the higher principle governs and confers status on the lower, makes the lower operative or gives it agency, as when bishops ordain a priest or grant a priest an office or place in the diocese. The higher authority makes the lower reality *come into being* in the relevant way and attain status and efficacy of its own. The enchanted universe fits easily with a hierarchical sociality and the distinction between the clergy and laity. Not only does the hierarchy have a certain office or function with respect to mediation—only the priest can confect the Eucharist—but the counsels of perfection indicate a "higher speed" or greater expectation of holiness and rigor for the consecrated than for the laity.

Not, however, if selves are buffered and objects cannot be charged with power. If we are buffered selves existing in a universe rather than in a cosmos, then mediation and hierarchy disappear along with "speeds" of holiness. This is the "age of Reform," according to Taylor, in which he includes but goes beyond the Protestant Reformation. On the one hand, this all fits neatly with the Reformation that, Taylor correctly notes, is far less about the authority of Scripture or the doctrine of justification than the diminution of the Eucharist. If the Eucharist is the real presence—body, blood, soul, and divinity of Jesus Christ—then at least one object in the world is charged, even super-saturated. If objects are charged then the self is not buffered and mediation and hierarchy are operative, the source of "white magic" necessitating status for the Church and her officers. If, however, the Eucharist is not the source and summit of the Christian life but merely a sign without efficacy, no "magic" exists and no use for mediation or hierarchy either. The goal, though, is not doctrinal; the real purpose is social reform. If priests and bishops and popes have no "magic," then all believers, and eventually all people, are capable, even required, to operate at the same higher speed of natural and moral capacity. Obviously, the idea that all people regardless of belief or baptism will operate at the higher speed indicates a merely natural project. Grace will wane and disappear, replaced by education, enlightenment, art, the state, or whatever other means of human elevation suffice to take the role previously held by grace and the sacraments. Chesterton somewhere quipped that knocking off the pope's miter also knocked off his head, meaning that the loss of religion resulted in the loss of reason, but we might also say that knocking off the miter removed the necessity of grace. Oddly, despite the Protestant insistence on *sola gratia*—grace alone—the rejection of mediation and hierarchy was the death knell for the necessity of grace. Human projects, merely human projects, all-too-human projects, would suffice to raise us all to equal righteousness, justice, and moral obligation. Overcoming the two-speed world required overcoming grace and all its trappings and paraphernalia, especially the Eucharist.

This is disenchantment, a rejection of special or uniquely charged things—sacraments and sacramentals—and the concomitant denial that people can be charged, either as agents (priests, bishops, popes) or as patients (the baptized, the communicant, the confirmand, the married). Overcoming hierarchy requires undoing mediation; undoing mediation requires disenchantment; disenchantment necessitates the universe of matter in motion rather than the cosmos. All this is to say that Christian theism devolved to deism, albeit of a providential sort. God exists, the deists claim, to set the laws of nature into motion... and then disappears. God remains a logical necessity, but He might as well be dead, and soon will be; He didn't do anything and wasn't in any way active in the world except by abstract providence, meaning the laws of nature as known to rationality. Once the Eucharist and its conditions of possibility are removed—a charged universe, porous selves, mediation, and hierarchy—the conception of God shrinks as He distances from us. He exists, He wants our good, and creates a universe allowing for our good, but the impersonal order of the universe turns out to be the most salient fact. Christian theism insists that God involves Himself with us because God desires more than merely natural flourishing for us— He wants us to know and love Him forever, He wants us to be His adopted sons, partakers of the divine nature.

Deism presents a God safely removed, and concerned only for our natural, human happiness. This results, as Taylor suggests, in "the eclipse of grace," since the "order God designed was there for reason to see" and "by reason and discipline" alone could humans "realize" their own flourishing. Reason and the laws of nature provide all necessary means to attain our good, "and this can be read from the design of our nature, [and] no further mystery can hide here." Deism, still committed to the existence of some sort of God, however far removed, finds it all too easy to simplify matters and commit to an impersonal order knowable, predictable, and to some extent controllable, by human reason and ingenuity. God adds nothing, and human experience becomes a god-like instrument within the forces of the universe. But we are free of God, free to make of ourselves what we wish.

## The Immanent Frame

I'm condensing Taylor's very long and complicated argument, the point of which is to explain the background conditions of belief, including how we view possibilities in the world. With this, Taylor's idea of non-exclusive humanism becomes plausible. If we take humanism to mean simply a concern for human fulfillment and the full human possibility there is no reason religious belief, at least of certain kinds, cannot be a humanism the glory of God is man fully alive, after all, to quote Irenaeus. Still, it never occurs to Irenaeus to think that the human is fully alive without relation to God, let alone that natural human flourishing excludes relation with God. Exclusive humanism, on the other hand, sees natural human flourishing as the exclusive possibility. There is no supernatural happiness to worry about, only immanent, temporal well-being. We're capable of providing clean water, clean energy, and clear skin, and those are the *only* reasonable concerns. Food, water, education, technology, GDP, political justice, and the next generation of iPhones or electric cars all make sense for us to create, and we will, if we are smart. Care for the beyond and the afterlife are pointless wastes of time at best, even impediments to progress; efforts for virtue, righteousness, or holiness are meaningful only with respect to individual health and happiness or social cohesion and progress. Nothing more.

Consequently, moderns—even those with religious belief —live and move and have their being within the *immanent frame*. Reality is imagined as a picture frame, or, better, reality is imagined as what is *inside* a picture frame, with the frame acting to limit our imagination and interests. Reality is immanentized, as is eschatology, with "paradise" reduced to peace, order, and good government, albeit with ample provisions, entertainments, and autonomy. Hope is for inner-worldly fulfillment, inner-worldly flourishing, and inner-worldly justice. Further, since the immanent frame has become *the* frame of our imagination, even traditional religious believers start from the immanent frame; it forms the conditions of belief. Perhaps one breaks on through to the other side, but the immanent remains the referent and starting-point. Immanence is obvious and manifest, as are the needs, sufferings, and delights of immanence; most modern people think so and are content within that frame. Transcendence? Not so obvious anymore, or not to many; just one option among many, and somewhat odd at that.

Taylor sharply distinguishes between secularity as a loss of religious observance and secularity as the background condition of belief. The distinction allows him to reject the familiar secularization thesis suggesting that as we get smart and educated we simply will stop believing in fairy tales. That's simplistic to the extreme, but secularity as a condition of belief, the context in which a person has or does not have faith, explains why people can maintain religious commitment *and* be secular in the sense that they believe *from within the immanent frame.* Immanence is the starting point of the modern mind, the basis of hopes and fears, the basis even of faith.

The immanent frame can be experienced in different ways. Immanence certainly is experienced by many from the standpoint of a *closed-world structure.* That is, not only do we begin within immanence, we end within immanence; the frame cannot be pierced or traversed. This life is all there is. This closed-world structure brings with it, not necessarily but commonly, an experience of malaise, somewhat oddly, given the successes of modernity. As Taylor says, moderns have a "sense of power, of capacity, in being able to order our world and ourselves," including "a sense of invulnerability." A disenchanted world frees us from having to cope with spirits and gods and forces beyond our control, so we are free of the anxieties of the porous self. We can't be harmed. On the other hand, the disenchanted world, by definition, possesses no intrinsic meaning, direction, or purpose. It is flat and empty, lacking the fullness of the medieval understanding. Lacking purpose, Taylor suggests people quite naturally find themselves experiencing melancholy, *ennui*, or acedia.[2]

While the conditions of belief have changed so that many people no longer believe, the West is haunted by belief. Believers experience their own religious commitment from within the immanent frame, perhaps, but unbelievers experience the remnants and remembrance of faith—and its security and stability. Unbelief is fragile; not only *might* there be more to life than immanence, we might desire an eternal reality beyond our transient efforts. Something has been lost, and something is known to have been lost. However much we accomplish and attain, however much we invent and discover, however many fires the modern Prometheus builds, it's unclear why it matters in any way. Life is thin, flat, without substance or depth. All will die and disappear, as if it never was, and the universe simply doesn't care if it was or not. The absence of God constitutes a vacuum, a threat. We have many options available to us, and people experiment with ersatz forms of religion as spiritual tourism, as a posture or pose rather than consent to something thought true and normative. Made-up

---

[2] I wrote on this more extensively in *Acedia and Its Discontents: Metaphysical Boredom in an Empire of Desire* (Kettering, OH: Angelico Press, 2015).

spirituality might console, perhaps even edify, but when known to be entirely concocted it's a shell identity, a bit of fashion worn for selfies but soon discarded for another ready-made, consumed identity: *inanis et vacua*. Modernity has its malaises, and is often experienced the way Olga experiences herself locked in her flat. No way out, no communication in or out, no lifeline, surrounded by death; with no Father to save.

## *An Open Possibility*

It is not that the immanent frame necessitates closed-world structures and malaise. According to Taylor, moderns also experience the immanent frame as the condition of belief and nevertheless believe. Immanence allows for closed-world structures but does not foreclose the possibility of open-world structures: the immanent frame "permits closure, without demanding it." A closed world—radical immanence—is not self-evident. It is not simply the way things are. Secularity does not arise because we have grown up, shed our adolescent, medieval faith, and entered into an adulthood with eyes wide open. Not at all. A closed-world structure is *chosen* and *constructed*. It is an interpretation, a story, a version of how the immanent frame might be experienced and understood, but it is in no way rationally self-evident.

The closed world is not a logical or rational conclusion from philosophical or scientific argument so much as a moral stance, an ethical commitment. It is, Taylor claims, self-deception and delusion to think that reason demands secularity—it does not. Instead secularity is demanded by a commitment to certain "'values,' virtues, excellences" of the sort especially welcome to the "independent, disengaged subject" who prefers an ethic of "independence, self-control, and self-responsibility." Secularity is a choice for the human being who thinks it better to have the "courage" to refuse the "easy comforts of conformity to authority, of the consolations of an enchanted world." This choice is buttressed by disenchanting tendencies, but it is not necessitated.

Or, as Taylor suggests, secularity of the closed-world structure is a kind of *faith*. Faith in the way the world *should be* if humans are *to be* the way they *wish* to be. It is, in his words, *faith* which ultimately determines if a particular individual or society will commit to an open or closed stance, but both "involve a step beyond available reasons into the realm of anticipatory confidence." Here I quibble, although I think my quibble worthwhile. Taylor should suggest that this anticipatory confidence is a version of hope rather than faith. Faith, suggests Peter Geach, is "assent to dogma given by an authority."[3] It is a commitment to certain truth claims, a judgment that things are true, and an act of the intellect. Faith sometimes finds it necessary to "hang on to a belief" in the face of confusion or temptation or doubt, but in those moments it is a hanging-on to a truth once known and affirmed by the intellect. If Taylor is correct in claiming, and I think it very likely he is, that secularity of the closed world *is not* a rational truth claim so much as an anticipatory confidence that certain values and virtues, a certain picture of human fulfillment, is in fact desirable and good, then it sounds much more like a version of hope than of faith.

---

[3] Cited in my essay "Hang On! Faith and Sexual Ethics," *Public Discourse* (October 11, 2022).

Hope, according to the *Catechism of the Catholic Church*, is that theological virtue by which we "desire the kingdom of heaven . . . as our happiness," and it responds "to the aspiration to happiness." It "takes up the hopes that inspire men's activities and purifies them so as to order them to the Kingdom of Heaven."[4] Now, I'm certainly not suggesting that the anticipatory confidence of the secularists of closed-world structures is genuine hope, the real theological virtue, or a gift of the Holy Spirit. Not at all. I am, though, suggesting that it is an ersatz version of hope. If hope desires happiness and responds to our aspiration to happiness, confident in "the help of grace," then confidence in the value of the closed world where humans can actualize their own well-being and flourishing through their own action and technique is a parasitic version of hope.

---

[4] *Catechism of the Catholic Church*, 1817–18.

# 3

# Malaises of Mastery

IN TAYLOR'S HISTORY, the age of Reform is marked by confidence. Humanity can finally overcome the anxiety of porousness and the threat of reality outside our control. We finally stride boldly into the world as agents and protagonists. Or such is the conceit. This attitude is well described by Yuval Noah Harari in *Homo Deus: A Brief History of Tomorrow*, although Harari cautions against its hubris:

> At the dawn of the third millennium, humanity wakes up, stretching its limbs and rubbing its eyes. . . . "Let's see what's on the agenda today."
> For thousands of years the answer to this question remained unchanged. . . . Famine, plague and war were always on the top of the list. For generation after generation humans have prayed to every god, angel and saint, and have invented countless tools, institutions and social systems—but they continued to die in their millions from starvation, epidemics and violence. . . . Yet at the dawn of the third millennium . . . we have managed to rein in famine, plague and war.[1]

---

[1] Yuval Noah Harari, *Homo Deus: A Brief History of Tomorrow* (New York: Harper, 2017), 1.

Problems remain, of course, but when we fail to solve them "we no longer shrug our shoulders and say, 'Well, that's the way things work in our imperfect world' or 'God's will be done.'" Instead, we "feel that somebody must have screwed up, we set up a commission of inquiry, and promise ourselves that next time we'll do better." And, he insists, we get results: famine, plague, and war are all on the decline, and when the system fails it is because of human error, not cosmic forces. Everything—*everything!*—is within our control. Even death, as he remarks elsewhere, is entirely optional, just a glitch of hardware resolvable in principle rather than an intractable problem, let alone an edict of God.[2] Everything is up to us, even death, once we refuse to conclude that "it is just the way it is," or "the will of God." Adults take charge; children look for absent fathers to save them.

This fits an oft-told account of humanism, the Enlightenment, and progress. In fact, the story is thought so obvious that it serves as default history. In that light, Taylor's differentiation between closed and open secularity is viewed as surprising, a challenge. Indeed, he describes *A Secular Age* as "making a continuing polemic" against "subtraction stories" where humans "liberated themselves" from earlier, confining worldviews; a necessary polemic against a deeply entrenched story of our confident maturity.[3]

This story overlooks the vertigo and confusion experienced by the early moderns as they lost confidence in the cosmos and creation. Rather than a sense of bold maturity, striding forward into the world as adults, they experienced

---

[2] Yuval Noah Harari and Daniel Kahneman, "Death Is Optional: A Conversation," *Edge* (March 4, 2015).

[3] Taylor, *Secular Age*, 22.

fragmentation and malaise, as Taylor reminds us. Luc Ferry suggests early modern physics "annihilated" the ancient-medieval world picture, offering "a field of forces and objects jostling for place without harmony."[4] Not only was the cosmos lost, but humans lost their place as well. The "harmonious frame of human existence . . . simply evaporated," leaving "the intellects of the time in a state of confusion it is virtually impossible for us to imagine today." They found themselves in an abyss, in a world lacking a horizon to distinguish up from down in any meaningful way. The "immediate effect of the Copernican revolution," as a famous essay by Alexander Koyré noted, "was to spread skepticism and bewilderment."[5]

## Humans without Image

The bewilderment was total, distorting and confusing every aspect of human concern, not merely the scientific. As Hans Jonas argued, the modern person was in crisis, for science declared itself "triumphant" over revelation without providing resources to guide our ultimate concerns: "Reason disqualified *itself* from that office. . . ." The ability to act became untethered from reason, and it was reason that abandoned itself *through* a triumphalist science in "the great Nothing."[6]

Jonas identifies three aspects of early modern thought prompting a subsequent nihilism. First, the replacement of

[4] Ferry, *Brief History of Thought*, 94.

[5] Koyré, "From the Closed World to the Infinite Universe," quotations in Ferry, 96.

[6] Hans Jonas, *Philosophical Essays: From Ancient Creed to Technological Man* (Englewood Cliffs, NJ: Prentice-Hall, 1974), 168. Quotes in the next several pages are from Jonas, 168–72.

creation with nature. While a created world is grounded in the intellect and will of a transcendent other, a universe self-constructs through forces internal to it. The world cannot be measured or judged by anything external, but neither is its current state the final word, for things will change as those forces develop. Consequently, science is entirely indifferent to the meaning of good, bad, perfect, imperfect, noble, or base. None of these terms correspond to anything in the universe; it is "a world of fact alien to value." Nothing is known about value in the world of nature and the methods by which nature is studied. The vacuum of goodness also removes all reference to God's goodness manifest in the world. The world is one of stark, valueless force; forces exist, and we can predict and (sometimes) control them, but without reference to natural purpose or ends. No intentionality or directedness can be ascertained in the world, resulting in the odd fact that the human being— also viewed naturalistically as no more than nature having risen to the level of consciousness—is "the sole repository" of intentions and ends, possessing an "ultimate monopoly on intention and goal."

Why are humans qualified to hold such a monopoly? What justifies our intentions as true or good? Also, as natural ourselves, with nature bereft of intention, is it the case that what appears to us as purpose and deliberation is simulacrum, a cosmic joke whereby entirely natural forces produce a false sense of freedom? Do we spend our lives asking, "who am I?" and "what ought I do?" even though such questions presuppose a world quite unlike the one we occupy? What sort of jest would it be if the universe spun off our anxious cares for no reason?

Second, not only the goodness of the universe vanishes

but also the old anthropology. According to Jonas, if God did not create us, we certainly cannot be said to be created in His image; we emerge from natural forces beyond good and evil. The very notion of human nature is suspect, beholden to a quasi-Platonic sense of an essential cause preserving a stable humanity. The universe cannot guarantee a universal, fixed human nature, however, since directionless force constantly making and remaking itself confers nothing stable. We have biological "becoming," the way we are *for now*, which is entirely accidental and changeable. Without a transcendent source, no permanent reality persists, let alone moral legitimacy or dignity of humans—we are left with "an 'image-less' image of man." Our ethics must change as well; it makes little sense to valorize human flourishing (as in Aristotle), or living according to nature (as in the Stoics), or right reason (as in Thomas Aquinas). What remains? *Be successful*, as a blind evolutionary imperative.

With essence usurped by becoming, history supplants ethics. As "a product of nature and its accidents," we are "the continuous product of . . . history and its man-made creations, i.e., of the different and changing cultures, each of which generates and imposes its own *values*—as matters of fact, not of truth." History, or better, *historicity* or *historicism*, lacks categories of objectivity, truth, legitimacy, validity, or universality. Even if historical forms of thought use such terms, they mean only *within* their confines, never beyond. It is more accurate to conclude there "*are* only matters of fact," and "as facts are mutable, so are values. . . . There is no appeal from the stream of fact to a court of truth" in ethics—not anymore.

Confusion and skepticism relentlessly continue, third, in what Jonas calls the "finishing touch" of psychology. In modern psychology the human is understood as detritus of the universe, it is a "cutting man down to size and stripping him in his own eyes of every vestige of metaphysical dignity." The human being is bereft of the image of God, lacking even a stable nature, a product of evolutionary and historicized forces; all candidates for a higher aspect of human nature, something beyond the animal or biological, are easily unmasked: critiqued, deconstructed, problematized, contextualized. Everything, including reason, is a "roundabout way of gratification for the most elementary, essentially base drives, out of which the complex, sophisticated psychic system of civilized man is ultimately constructed and by whose energies alone it is moved." The "higher" is not different in kind from the "lower," but merely a fact without normative meaning or value. The great paradox of the modern condition is that the reduction

> of man's stature, the utter humbling of his metaphysical pride, goes hand in hand with his promotion to quasi-God-like privilege and power. The emphasis is on *power*. For it is not only that he now holds the monopoly on value in a world evacuated of values; that as the sole source of meaning he finds himself the sovereign author and judge of his own preferences with no heed to an eternal order.[7]

Reason, or a version of reason, displaced revelation without supplying a replacement. Modernity stripped itself of ethics—and even, somewhat oddly, weakened reason through the dissolving power of reason, while confidently asserting that revelation had lost authority. As Luc Ferry puts it,

[7] Ibid., 172.

modernity released an acid on the world, a solvent that could not be contained before turning on itself, dissolving its own claims and pretensions, leaving only force and power, revealing everything as base and elemental.[8] It consumed itself, and the human along with it.

## *Tyranny of Mastery*

Bill McClay explores a paradox implicit in the progressive "belief that the infirmities of the human condition were no longer a permanent given, but lay within the human agency to alter; and that the march of scientific knowledge . . . was granting human beings an ever-expanding power to control their circumstances."[9] Such optimism entailed a commitment to human mastery—we are captains of our souls, we are masters of our fates. Ours (supposedly) is a time of confidence, of triumph, with human destiny and even the forces of evolution and history now within our schemes and plans.

The best-laid plans often fail. We're well aware of a sense of anxiety and mood of crisis in our own moment: financial crisis, environmental crisis, demographic crisis, climate crisis, and more, an endless litany. McClay suggests it is not failure but the success of mastery lurking behind our unease. Mastery suggests responsibility. The maxim "ought implies can" indicates that whatever is beyond our control places no moral obligations on us. I cannot will myself not to feel hunger, so it would be meaningless to demand I feel no pangs on a fast day. I can choose not to eat, despite my feelings of hunger, so fasts can be obligatory, but it would

[8] Ferry, *Brief History of Thought*, 144–45.
[9] Wilfred McClay, "The Illusion of Mastery: Man and Authority," *The City* (Spring 2011): 20–30, at 20.

be nonsense to demand I control appetite. In the ideology of mastery the maxim reverses: no longer "ought implies can" but "can implies ought." If it is possible, say, to limit suffering then we *ought* to do so. If it is possible to provide food and housing for the needy, we are obligated. If it is possible to admit immigrants and refugees, then it is a moral crime not to do so. And so on.

Note, however, that the idea of mastery and its duties contains no limiting principle. If it is possible to end famine, plague, and war, then we must. Right! Since we are able to test for genetic abnormalities of the child in utero and thereby "cure" Down syndrome, and can implies ought, then we ought to end Down syndrome. Right? Right![10] Or, we now have the power to edit genes to control human evolution and better our lot—ought we do so? Well… the logic follows. As McClay puts it, mastery places terrible responsibility on us, particularly in a world without God. Without "acts of God" or "fate" or "providence" to accept, this bad thing *could have been* prevented with better planning or technology or technique; since it could have been it *ought to have been*, and *somebody is at fault*. Someone is to be blamed.

If someone is always blameworthy, mastery brings anxiety in its wake. We know that someone—perhaps me— deserves blame. Of course we do not actually have mastery over all things, nor reasonably expect to possess such power; this account of mastery is ideology, says McClay, a

[10] Down syndrome has all but disappeared in Iceland, for instance, where prenatal screening results in nearly 100 percent of such pregnancies ending in abortion. In the words of one report, this leads to "eradicating Down syndrome." See Julian Quinones and Arijeta Lajka, "What kind of society do you want to live in? Inside the country where Down syndrome is disappearing," *CBS News* (August 15, 2017).

tyranny, and the illusion of mastery makes the tyranny that much worse. We are "'too smart' to fall for the idea that anything is truly beyond the reach of human agency, and that calling something 'God's will' is anything more than rank mystification." Instead, we have scapegoats, but since much of what happens is within our particular agency, the scapegoat will often be ourselves. The old question of who sinned so that this man is blind will never again be answered with the oddly comforting response, "no one; rather that the works of God be manifest" (John 9:3–4).

Even death is optional, chosen rather than awaited. Some interpret this as ultimate agency, the final autonomy of self-(dis)possession, and tendentiously call it death with dignity. Conversely, it also means that cancer, or a car accident, is in some way deserved, something to condemn rather than endure. We need not suffer the fear of death only—perhaps a human constant—but also culpability for death, and all manner of anxiety accompanies responsibility—thus "safetyism." Mastery promised to transform us into supermen, but the "typical man of the medical-miracle future will not be an Übermensch. He will be more like an obsessive-compulsive handwasher who lives in constant dread of other people's germs and ends up living the life of a wealthy hermit. . . ."

## Humanitarian Dreams

In addition to scientific and technological mastery, modernity's pretensions included hopes for perpetual peace and universal humanitarianism. The idea of a common humanity is neither unique to nor invented by modernity, but it is fundamentally transformed by it. Already the Roman empire coupled with Stoic thought envisioned cosmopolitan reason.[11] The Christian Church altered this, understanding itself as a universal community rather than an empire. Ancient thought acknowledged a shared human nature but viewed regional communities as distinct, and even the empire did not conceive of itself as a single community. The Church, however, viewed itself as a real community open to all human beings, including those long dead and those yet to be born. Catholicity—universality—was essential to its self-understanding.

The wars of religion, the Reformation, the apparent inability of Christianity to take root in parts of Asia, and the failure of the Church to provide anything like adequate political governance convinced many European thinkers that the Church could not meet its universal aspirations, but no other political form seemed adequate either. Thus emerged, suggests Pierre Manent, the idea of "founding the universal on humanity alone." A single subject—humanity—despite the particular instantiations in various languages, histories, and political societies, allowed a universal vision, however abstract and ethereal. Christianity would be replaced by Humanity, a new religious object of veneration, and with a new eschatology as well, defined by "the recognition and adoration of itself." Odd, especially once science cast the Aristotelian understanding of a shared human essence into doubt—a vision of shared humanity without metaphysical basis.

People belong to different races or nations, but humanity recognizes humanity in the other and venerates humanity.

---

[11] This section draws upon the work of Pierre Manent, *The Religion of Humanity: The Illusion of Our Times*, trans. Paul Seaton (South Bend, IN: St. Augustine's Press, 2022), esp. 30–49.

Concord and respect ought to follow. Particular differences—race, sex, language, heritage, history, creed—slink
to the background as we labor for the good of humanity,
which includes all. The limits of political bond and affection are shuttled offstage and abstract affection should overcome all limits to care for others. The new humanitarian
grants no legitimacy to our frail capacities but fantasizes a
common humanity without particular and finite mediation
of political communities and their histories. We shall be citizens of the world.

Utopia should be easy, requiring no more than a recognition of ourselves in each other. It can be done, and thus
ought to be done, and ought to be done *immediately.*
Manent, himself a defender of the nation-state as the most
reasonable of political forms, notes the absence of patience
or political prudence evident in this dream; if the "humanity of the other person" is "self-evident" and it is a great
affront to not immediately recognize this fact. Humanitarianism differs dramatically from the Christian duty to recognize a common creator and common redeemer of all
human beings, however much some attempt to conflate the
Christian and humanitarian visions. Christianity asks for
love of neighbor, and is universally inclusive in its definition
of neighbor, but asks us to love neighbors *not* for their own
sake but for love of God. The neighbor is loved because
God is to be loved, and it is God who has created the neighbor in His own image; the neighbor is loved as an image of
God, not in merely human recognition. Since we have a
common redeemer, the Second Adam who offers salvation
to all, and in whom our identity is caught up and hidden
(Col 3:3), we love the other in Christ, through Christ, and
with Christ. ("Through him, with him, and in him," in the

words of the Concluding Doxology of the Mass.) The Church asks us to see all persons *as other Christs*, and to love them as such. Furthermore, the love with which we love is a grace—*caritas* is not mere "fellow feeling"; the "love of God is poured forth in our hearts by the Holy Spirit" (Rom 5:5).

Manent suggests that genuine charity for fellow humans requires not only love of God but love of the "true God" within the mediation of His body on earth, the Church. The universal Christian aspiration is limitless in principle, open to and directed to all, but also instantiated and particularized by and within the true Church, which does not contain all people. The religion of humanity, conversely, claims to enable and command—can implies ought, after all—a version of charity not only distinct and independent of the Church, but actually critical of, and hostile to, it and its particular mediation of charity. Further, since the religion of humanity now exists and governs, any return to the Christian vision must be viewed as a narrowing of charity, and thus retrograde, regressive. Either the Church embraces the religion of humanity, or the Church must of necessity be viewed as a benighted enemy. As Ryszard Legutko notes, the humanitarian impulse claims everything, including religion, and any attempt to persist outside the new religion must be "outdated, backward-looking, useless, but at the same time extremely dangerous as preserving the remnants. . . . Some may be tolerated for some time, but . . . should be treated with the harshness they deserve."[12]

Manent asks a hard question: it's not difficult to concep-

[12] Ryszard Legutko, *The Demon in Democracy: Totalitarian Temptations in Free Societies*, trans. Teresa Adelson (New York: Encounter Books, 2016), 21.

tualize the humanitarian dream of *extension*—the community of humanity extended to all—but what is its *intension*, or content? Everyone is included, but in what, precisely? Perhaps a concern for suffering, with content provided by pity, although this soon requires (or is seen to require) extending humanity to animals, but, still, there is *no content* to pity, it tells us *nothing* about the *substance* of inclusion. Humanity includes all humans, but a humanity without content.

Manent pivots to a remarkable claim, one making sense of the babel of our time. He notes that moderns did not invent the idea of the human, since the Greeks knew barbarians were human but distinct because living outside the *polis*. "Barbarian" was a political classification, not a literal "dehumanization," although stressing difference. For Comte and theorists of modern humanity, on the other hand, the denial of difference is the order of the day. If we have both sentiment for our fellows *and* the technical mastery to accomplish our desires, the age-old human tendency to seek good and avoid evil will be resolved, albeit oddly. Altruism (and I would add mastery) will achieve goodness, and "there will be no reason for any flight from evil." Evil will not exist and there will be nothing to avoid. Desire for the good "will be necessarily lukewarm as well, since it will already be essentially satisfied." The new religion inevitably loses its motive force—seek good, avoid evil—and collapses on itself. The "reunited and reconciled humanity" seeks no good greater than itself, since there is no good to seek other than humanity, which it has already fulfilled. Thus humanitarianism—*qua* ideology, not *caritas*—succumbs to a dreary slumber and decadence. It possesses all the good it envisions, and there is nothing other than the immanent good to seek. Evil is overcome, and the activity of modern people will, of an inner logic of their own accomplished dreams, lose all force and potency. Masters, yes; gods of their own fashioning, yes; but also stupefied, bored, enervated, decadent, and insensible.

McClay concluded that mastery doesn't produce the Übermensch but a compulsive handwasher; similarly, Manent refers to Nietzsche when observing that modern power ends in enervation. "We have invented happiness," Manent quotes Nietzsche, not as the Übermensch but the Last Man who "no longer knows the meaning of the verbs 'to love,' 'to create,' or 'to long for,'" who "makes everything small."[13] A small, immanent room from which there is no escape.

Humanity, conscious of itself as final, with no good or evil to pursue or avoid, views the present generation as utterly superior to previous generations, with the past either irrelevant or erased. (Cancel culture and the tearing down of statues is not unexpected, for Manent or Nietzsche.) The current generation—now fully albeit boringly and anxiously human—excludes the past and its problems and thus "ceases to understand itself." It is satisfied, sated, complete in its self-congratulation, and essentially passive. Humanity, this great and now accomplished good, functions as an object of worship and contemplation but not a source of action, certainly not genuinely political action. Quoting Comte, Manent notes, "Humanity is made up of more dead than living," and "the dead increasingly govern the living." The living no longer govern themselves, at any rate.

---

[13] *Religion of Humanity*, 65, citing *Thus Spake Zarathustra*.

## *Paradoxes of Immanence*

In these three chapters I have explored the history and experience of immanence. For a variety of reasons the old sense of an enchanted universe no longer operates as the background condition of belief, even for religious people, and the immanent frame shapes the imagination of people of the developed, scientific world and determines their options. The forces of the world are not viewed as the threats to our safety our ancestors experienced, for humans are not thought of as porous, nor the world as charged, but selves are buffered and the world flattened. Freed from these threats, the modern person viewed the universe as perhaps put into motion by God, who however then disappeared from the scene and became irrelevant, replaced with the forces of the universe, all in principle understandable and even controllable through our mastery. With that power, however, a new anxiety emerges, not that of the porous self in a charged world, of course, but the terror of the confident, capable agent responsible for everything, unable either to rely on or to blame God, in a universe in which our acts ultimately mean nothing. These conditions prompt a sense of urgency and the live possibility to better man's lot, for everyone, and fast, in an endless cycle of reform and improvement, but in a humanitarian dream that lacks an obvious point or terminus.

Several paradoxes have emerged in these chapters, experienced by modern people as problems to overcome, although their attempts to do so are hampered by false versions of hope. First, disenchantment allows a new experience of freedom, security, and possibility for reform, but brings also emptiness, flatness, and pointlessness (what Taylor calls the malaise of modernity), calling into question the worth of freedom and security. Second, moderns have confidence in their ability to master their lot and fate, to control fortune, but the malaise of mastery results in a frenzy of anxiety and an exaggerated sense of responsibility. Third, moderns see things without superstition and with clearheaded realism; they take themselves to be the sole source of intentionality and value but at the same time ontological rubbish, an accident of the universe, their intentions random and without value. To summarize these three malaises: (1) immanence, (2) loss of value, and (3) failure of hope.

All this is to say that whatever the benefits of radical immanence, despair lurks in the wings; humans are trapped (some think) in immanence, without a sense of identity or purpose, without a sense that the universe cares if they exist or not, or that the universe matters, and without any ultimate transcendence to save them. No father, no God, to break down the door, open the lock, repair the telephone, or save his children from illness. Olga's confinement and madness are the malaise and immanence of our age.

Created in the image of God, with a supernatural vocation, humans are not well-suited to radical immanence, of course, and the despair of the situation is met with our own efforts to solve the dilemma, to bring something of the life of the non-immanent into immanence. And so many (1) "hope" in a frenzied activism, (2) posit the dreams of rationalism, or (3) tell enchanting fantasies, ignoring their unreality. That is, given the loss of religion and the ensuing despair, inner-worldly religions and false visions of hope emerge—the subject of the next three chapters.

# PART II

Idylls of Inner-Worldly Religion

# 4

## Denatured Activism

IN THE NEXT THREE chapters I explore three false visions of hope—humanitarianism, rationalism, and faux-enchantment. I understand their allure: they appear responsive to the moment and its irrationalities, including the paradoxes discussed in the previous chapters. Modern life is disenchanted; people find themselves trapped in anxiety by the tyranny of mastery; the immanent frame is narrow and stifling. The human intellect, prone to temptation, resists unintelligibility and looks to escape the cage, however gilded.

However attractive, these visions are nonetheless idylls, disappointing illusions. "Idyll" shares the same etymological root as "idol"—*eidos* (form, picture)—and it has something of a connotation of idolatry. In literature an idyll generally has a pastoral or rustic theme, as if to convey peace, ease, and contentment in a picturesque, bucolic setting. It's also somewhat inconsequential or unserious, fleeting, unsustainable, or likely to disappear. I mean it in the sense that British educator Charlotte Mason used in her critiques of educational systems.[1] In her understanding, an educational idyll is a system or method delivering lovely

---

[1] See Charlotte Mason, "Three Educational Idylls," *The Parents' Review* 23 (November, 1912): 801–11.

outcomes in the behavior or skills of children and so apparently effective and desirable, but conflating behavior with education and mistaking the appearance—a picturesque image—for the reality of an educated, dynamic, intelligent, self-directed child alive in the entirety of her being. Not only are appearances preferred over reality, but in time the mistaken emphases do injustice to the child by malforming her so that she too prefers appearance to the real. One sees this often, for a simple example, when a father delights in the apparently good behavior of his child—which, let's admit it, is highly desirable, and a relief—without concerning himself with her actual virtue. Many wicked people have impeccable social graces. Idylls mistake the form of a thing for its being, and in their concern for form distort reality, including the person. At the same time, the idyll is attractive, has a sweet allure, and can entrance and captivate, even as it quietly, inexorably, erodes the foundation of the human person.

In a time of chaos, with so much confusion and malaise, the idylls of humanitarianism, rationalism, and enchantment are understandable. These idylls promise something lovely and soothing, a salve to a frustrated and anxious moment, but they prefer the appearance to the reality and are ruinous. Like idols, they promise the security and power of the true God, but in the end serve only to diminish our humanity, deform our loves, and render us less than we might be. They are winsome theories, perhaps, yet detrimental to true human flourishing.

## Decapitated Reason

Plato's thought emerged against the backdrop of the political and spiritual disorder of Athens. Not only had Athens faltered in the Peloponnesian War, an external shock and mark of dysfunction, but Athens had killed Socrates, described by Plato in the closing words of the *Phaedo* as "the best, and also the wisest and the most upright," of men. While his crimes were supposedly impiety and corrupting the youth, he was actually killed, so Plato thought, for choosing philosophy over philodoxy; he loved wisdom rather than opinion, and in so doing called the ways of his own city into question.[2]

Athens, like all cities, was full of opinion (*doxa*) about all manner of things, including questions of everyday importance and discussion. What is good to do? How should the young be educated? What is just or unjust? What is friendship? How are we to be courageous? These are not especially arcane questions, as they affect everyone and everyone seems to have thoughts on them, although the reasonableness and truth of those opinions is contested. In some ways the contested nature of opinions regarding such matters just is what politics is about, and political theory nothing more than reflections on the truth and grounds of these opinions. As Eric Voegelin understands the matter, Socrates and Plato viewed political theory in the following way: was there an order, a pattern against which opinions about the good human being and good human action could be judged, or was subjective opinion all we had? Socrates questions those who claim to know the meaning of piety, courage, friendship, and so on, discovering that they did not have grounds for their claims but professed only custom or opinion.

---

[2] Until noted, I'm citing Eric Voegelin, *Modernity without Restraint: The Collected Works of Eric Voegelin*, Volume 5, ed. Manfred Henningsen (Columbia, MO: University of Missouri Press, 2000), 257–92, at 257.

Honest questioning, thus, conflicted with opinion, and not in a merely semantic sense: it cost Socrates his life, revealing to Plato the hollowness and spiritual disorder of Athens. The philosopher asked the same questions as everyone else, but sought the truth of things rather than words about things. Athens's condemnation of Socrates was an execution of questions, a condemnation of truth-seeking. Plato's writings are a defense of Socrates and a trial of Athens, for Plato was convinced that questioning—reason—could go beyond opinion to discover the truth about the order of being, and against that order of being Athens and its judgments were judged.

Genuine political theory began with the insight that the truth of being could be known from within the human experience. Human beings discovered in themselves a movement toward, a love and desire for, the "world-transcendent order of being." The philosopher sought to know transcendent order and was impelled by an order discerned and experienced in his own intellect. Questioning was not an idle pastime for the argumentative, nor mere cleverness, and certainly not gamesmanship, but a *philia*, a love, for the transcendent and divine source of being experienced from within the philosopher's own soul.

According to Voegelin, our time is marked by ideologies, all of which refuse or prohibit questioning in the Socratic-Platonic sense. This, he says, is not simply a love of opinion —all times and places have philodoxers—but a "conscious, deliberate, and painstakingly elaborated obstruction" of reason. This ideological obstruction of the force of reason lies behind so many of our political diseases, resulting in a socially approved deformation of the human.

Philosophy in the classical sense was not a list of beliefs, what people mean when they ask, "what is your philosophy?" and assume you will respond with a list of propositions or dogmas. Instead, philosophy was "man's responsive pursuit of his questioning unrest to the divine source that aroused it."[3] Reason, *nous*, is the place of this existential tension, and reason which is open to that tension and the ground of that tension is properly ordered, in keeping with the truth of being and the truth of being human. The *philia* of philosophy is not the curiosity of academic specialists but ordered to the transcendent ground of being. As a result, those who are closed to it turn away in alienation from their own self: "alienation is a withdrawal from the humanity that is constituted by the tension toward the ground." Voegelin calls this a "pathological derailment," a "disease" of the soul, a "psychopathology." As understood by the classical tradition, the tension of our existence, our unrest, is joyful because "the questioning has direction; the unrest is experienced as the beginning of the theophanic event in which the *nous* reveals itself as the divine ordering force in the *psyche* of the questioner and the cosmos at large." To lose the pull of the transcendent, to lose the joyful unrest pulling us to the divine, is to lose humanity. To forbid questioning, as ideology does, is wanton destruction of the human.

Many have lost such joyful unrest. Many view themselves and reason as fundamentally closed off, as operating in an "inner-worldly way" without "permeation from the highest source."[4] In the immanent frame, the cares and

---

[3] Citations are from "Reason: The Classic Experience," in *Anamnesis,* trans. Gerhart Niemeyer (Columbia, MO: University of Missouri Press, 1978), 89–115, at 96.

[4] Citations are from Voegelin, *Modernity without Restraint,* 59–69.

content of the world can exhaust the scope of reality, drowning out the pull of reason and the divine order, but as Voegelin insists, we "cannot annul the human condition itself." Inner-worldly realities will become "new gods." Older sacred symbols will be replaced by the inner-worldly, with sacral qualities of their own; genuine religion will be replaced by ersatz varieties; eschatological visions of "a transcendent community of the spirit" replaced by "an earthly condition of perfected humanity."

The inner-worldly religion of human progress is ideological: when unable to survive analysis or questioning it redefines the meaning of truth itself. The perfection of humanity takes on a mythic status, beyond question, treated as self-evident and valued by all right-thinking people. Ideological faith cannot be disrupted, even though it requires, as Voegelin suggests, the decapitation of God so as to allow the new "holy purpose" of inner-worldly perfection. Not merely God is decapitated, though, since evacuating the transcendent source and object of our questioning decapitates and deforms *us* as well.

## Denatured Nature

One way, perhaps a primary way, in which humans decapitate themselves is by denaturing humanity. In an earlier chapter I discussed the move from creation to nature and the implications as goodness is replaced by force and humans diminished to ontological rubbish, meat robots in a cold universe, even as the religion of humanity springs up. But nature itself suffers the solvent of modernity—from creation to nature, and from nature to the vacuum. *Inanis et vacua*, albeit in the guise of and in service of humanity.

In the older Platonic-Aristotelian-Thomistic worldview,

humans share a nature and thus a common fulfillment. Any entity is what it is—this sort of thing rather than that sort of thing—because it has form or essence as its principle of intelligibility. All things seek their own act or fulfillment, and since nothing other than God is fully act and fully itself, natural entities must develop through an internal source of motion or change toward their finality or perfection. An acorn, if undamaged and given such necessary external conditions as soil, water, and sunlight, naturally develops into a mature tree. Likewise humans by nature seek those perfections proper to rational animals. As substance we naturally seek existence; as animals we seek to preserve and augment our lives and to reproduce; as rational we seek friends, a polity, knowledge, and truth about the divine ground; furthermore, as rational we seek the lower aspects of our flourishing in a rational way, so that we do not simply reproduce but marry and educate offspring, do not simply eat but dine, and do not seek a mere alliance but a polity for the common good. We do all this by nature.

Unlike the acorn, humans are persons. We are not simply "whats" defined by essence but "whos" relating to our essence through freedom and self-directedness. It is our reasonable and natural good to reproduce in the context of marriage, but it is obviously possible to act sexually in a variety of non-marital ways. It is our natural good to seek the divine ground, but we can choose idolatry, innerworldly religion, and so on. We cannot replace or eradicate our nature—it is just what we are—but as persons we can and do have the power to relate to our nature in virtuous or vicious ways, in reasonable or unreasonable ways. Persons are responsible for their own self-directedness within the outlines of nature, and we can develop ourselves towards either fulfillment or damnation (in both temporal and eternal versions). God governs through providence, but providence includes *how* God has created, and he has created us as persons. The usual manner in which God governs us is through our own self-governance, through our own reason and will, although our reason participates in the divine reason and is not invented whole-cloth.

Since we are responsible for the attainment of our good, we have the obligation to seek it in a reasonable and virtuous way. Given our obligations, we have rights to direct ourselves. For example, because I have the duty to educate and rear my children, I have the right to educate and rear my children, which is why parents are primary educators (as articulated by the Catholic Church) and why parents give permission or license to schools or to the state to educate, but not the other way around. Another example: we have the duty to seek the truth about God and to live in keeping with that truth, which is why there are rights of conscience and religious freedoms the state ought to respect, secure, and nurture. Even God does not do violence to our will, and while we cannot attain salvation without the grace and work of God, he does not save us without us, and never by irresistible grace without our free cooperation.

Rights, in other words, have their ground in duties; duties have their ground in our goods; and goods have their ground in our nature. Rights, thus, have their foundation in human nature, and natural rights are an articulation of what by nature we are obligated by reason to seek. Or such was the traditional understanding. No more. *Natural rights* are increasingly viewed as a threat to human dignity and replaced with a denatured vision of *human rights*.

Human rights are thought to be universal, held by all humans whatever their other differences, but based on equality rather than nature. Equality, however, is thought to be jeopardized by judgments about morality or about the good. If there are natural goods, then there are virtuous or reasonable ways of attaining those natural goods, implying there are bad or vicious actions and bad or vicious people. Such judgments are thought to violate the commitments of the inner-worldly religion of humanity, however, and thus we have a complete reversal and return to the celebration and veneration of *opinion* in all its subjectivity and variation. The philosopher's questions, those seeking the ground of being and its normative truths, including the truths of human nature and human fulfillment, violate the religion of humanity and equality. Opinion is cherished, truth is not, for truth and moral judgment discriminate, suggesting some things are more and others less, some better and others worse.

Human rights, while universal in scope and extension, have almost no intension. They suppose no content, certainly not the content of human nature and the goods proper to our nature. The sole justification for human rights is their universality, not their truth, and they are universal only because they make no claims of genuine and grounded content. They are formless aspirations to equality rather than substantive claims about the good.[5] Lacking content while making demands for equality, human rights are cashed out

[5] Pierre Manent is very good on this subject; see especially the first chapter of *Natural Law and Human Rights: Toward a Recovery of Practical Reason*, trans. Ralph C. Hancock (South Bend, IN: University of Notre Dame Press, 2020), 1–18.

in terms of notions such as freedom, self-determination, choice, autonomy, and diversity—all fundamentally negative notions. Freedom is understood as the absence of limiting circumstances; self-determination, choice, and autonomy mean a lack of interference by others; diversity means non-conformity, non-uniformity. Equality means not much more than a refusal to judge or evaluate difference.

This is explicit rejection of natural rights. Natural rights have substance because linked to those goods proper to the fulfillment of our nature. Human rights, lacking substance or determination, largely provide no basis for practical judgments and concrete political determinations. Human rights depend on an impoverished, empty, denuded nature; a denatured nature, or a nature stripped bare of all content. But how are we to judge, or find motive for making particular practical judgments, in the absence of content? Our natural motives—and remember that nature is an internal source of motion or change, a substantial source of motive—are bracketed, erased, or viewed as a threat to humanity, but our motives then become formless and devoid of content.

Consequently, the political and moral motives of much of the West become negative. More choice (meaning fewer constraints) and more diversity (meaning less uniformity). The mode is one of undoing, taking apart, deconstructing, and critique, all in the name of emancipation, liberation, self-determination, and choice. While the old natural-rights tradition was fundamentally an articulation of natural law, the new understanding is law-less, for law is an ordering principle of reason by authority directing us to the good, and every aspect of that definition is in tension with formless human rights.

This goes some way towards explaining the seeming pointlessness of conversation and argument about rights. Not only are opinions valued as highly (perhaps higher) than the truth sought by philosophy but we are arguing about nothing, based on nothing. Consider arguments about sexual acts. In the older tradition the substance of the debate was based on a common human nature and common human good, with reasonable and unreasonable ways to accomplish that good. The sexual good was substantively understood as marital, with marital understood as reproductive in root capacity. This is contestable, of course, and was often honored in the breach, but the current debate has no content. In the contemporary realm, other than consent (meaning a lack of coercion or deceit) there is no human thing to discuss: "all one can say is that there is nothing to say, since it is a matter of indifference."

## Vacuous Speech

We should not be surprised to observe that political speech is often vacuous. Some of this can be blamed on media and the internet, but the underlying cause is the failure of speech itself. Although bizarre, an episode in C.S. Lewis's *That Hideous Strength* is relevant.[6] The scene is a formal banquet in luxurious settings, populated with luminaries from politics, the academy, entertainment—the sort of party one sees photographed in the "society" pages of the better newspapers. The meal is elegant, with the usual murmuring sounds of pleasantries and small talk punctured by the occasional bit of laughter and clattering of silverware on

---

[6] C.S. Lewis, *That Hideous Strength* (New York: Scribner, 2003).

china. As the dinnerware is cleared and the port served, the ritual after-dinner speech ensues.

As Lewis describes it: "For the first few minutes, anyone glancing down the long tables would have seen what we always see on such occasions . . . the patient faces of responsible but serious diners, who had long since learned how to pursue their own thoughts, while attending to the speech just enough to respond wherever a laugh or a low rumble of serious assent was obligatory." Then "a change" as "face after face look up and turn in the direction of the speaker," first with curiosity, incredulity, then "something between fascination and horror." The reason for this sudden attention is the odd behavior of Horace Jules, the speaker, something of a public intellectual and scientist—think Richard Dawkins—and Director of the National Institute of Coordinated Experiments, or N.I.C.E., which is hosting the evening. First he simply misspeaks, saying "Calvary" rather than "Cavalry," before uttering sentences with all the right intonations and cadence, but lacking content: the "future density of mankind depended on the implosion of the horses of Nature." Is he drunk, thinks one character? Am I hard of hearing, or perhaps myself intoxicated, thinks another, upon hearing Jules say, "the madrigore of verjuice must be talthibianised." Whatever does that mean?

One woman begins to laugh hysterically, prompting the master of ceremonies to stand up, interrupt Jules, authoritatively clear his throat to regain order, and pronounce in his deepest voice, "Tidies and fugleman." Whatever affected Jules has spread. Then laughter, shouting matches, and fights break out, and the noisy hubbub is pierced by screams as a tiger leaps into the room, having escaped from the animal-testing laboratories. Not just a tiger. Wolves, snakes, elephants, a gorilla, each maddened by the terror and frenzy of the diners—"they did not stop to eat what they killed, or not more than to take one lick of the blood. There were dead and dying bodies everywhere." And in the middle of the room, in that babel, stands a huge man (who turns out to be Merlin of all people—it is a strange story), loudly intoning, "*They that have despised the Word of God, from them shall the word of man also be taken away.*"

The West has rejected God, transcendence, and philosophy, and so it has lost the word as well, lost meaningful political speech. Manent explores how a common criticism of democracy was that it "multiplied words but was incapable of action," but now the resources allowing words to have substance are themselves dissolved.[7] Political speech has little tie to political action, he suggests, or at least is not a form of deliberation giving cause and substance to subsequent action. Instead, words are thought to constitute action, as evident in political correctness, woke culture, "slacktivism," and so on. Unpleasant speech, especially speech that seemingly degrades equality or humanity, is viewed as equivalent to the worst action. Meanwhile, action seems to just occur, performed by agencies and bureaucracies utterly nonresponsive to the citizenry. The speech of citizens and their representatives—while endless in some ways: think social media—is pointless and inactive, a distraction. Action, when it does happen, is wordless; it just happens without public deliberation, and so, in a sense, is *not* political action because the people did not debate, reflect, and argue as the

---

[7] Pierre Manent, *Metamorphoses of the City: On the Western Dynamic*, trans. Marc LePain (Cambridge, MA: Harvard University Press, 2013), 10.

condition of the act. We have neither political speech nor political act.

## *Smugglers*

In the American context, it is fair to place some blame for the degradation of political and moral speech on John Rawls, our most influential political theorist. I'm simplifying somewhat, although not unfairly, by stressing that Rawls asks citizens to bracket or ignore the things mattering most to them. Rawls suggests that in liberal society good citizens are those who do not appeal to reasons internal to their comprehensive viewpoints, such as a religion, but only to public reason. Now, it happens that comprehensive viewpoints often overlap or share certain commitments with other viewpoints, even if for different reasons. A Roman Catholic, an Orthodox Jew, and a Kantian might provide quite distinct reasons for the intrinsic value of a human being—Christ died for all, God created all, autonomy—while sharing the conclusion in an overlapping consensus, and thus the conclusion is part of public reason even though the particular rationales for the conclusion are not. Only public reason is to be used for political discourse, although Rawls grants full license for the particular communities to appeal to their own reason in their private affairs.

Other concepts from Rawls bracket even more of our knowledge, namely the *veil of ignorance* in the *original position*. In order to arrive at a commitment to justice as fairness, Rawls posits a thought experiment in which we know almost nothing about ourselves. We don't know our sex, race, looks, athletic abilities, family background, religious commitment, intelligence, and so on, for the temptation is always to favor oneself and one's own group. Since we don't know if any particular vision of justice would be favorable or unfavorable to us, we will be inclined, according to the theory, to choose neutral conceptions of justice applicable to everyone so as to not advantage others over ourselves. A kind of rational self-interest, one without any content of selfhood, moves us to choose and support an account of justice which in principle is acceptable to all, and would be accepted by all who engage in the thought experiment.

These ideas have received much scholarly commentary from many angles; my interest here is the narrowing and dimming of substance in deliberation and debate Rawls's theory all but guarantees. As Steven D. Smith notes, many political disagreements are rather straightforward, even if hotly contested, when the ends or purposes are held in common and only means are debated.[8] Everyone agrees that high inflation is economically ruinous, or that polluted tap water is undesirable, even if we disagree on whether to raise interest rates or provide national funding for local water treatment facilities. Such disputes allow for meaningful debate and the giving of reasons. Other disputes, however, concern the desirability of ends or goals themselves. Is same-sex marriage just or unjust? Is abortion a reproductive right or the illicit killing of a person? Here the disagreement is not about means or instruments but about good and bad, right and wrong—and substantive reason is barred from the discussion.

Rawls and his followers tend to view religion, metaphysics, and moral systems as conversation-stoppers rather than conversation-starters. If believers appeal to God's will in the debate about same-sex marriage, not only do they appeal to

---

[8] Steven D. Smith, *The Disenchantment of Secular Discourse* (Cambridge, MA: Harvard University Press, 2010), 211–12.

a source of authority the interlocutor doesn't grant—whose God are we talking about?—but their understanding of God's authority makes them intractable and uncompromising. From their perspective, they are unable to contravene the will of God and unable to make a political compromise, as would be done by public reason and its concerns with fairness. Wouldn't it be more conducive to public engagement and decision if we ignored such comprehensive commitments and started with that on which everyone in principle agrees? Religion is definitely not a source of universal agreement and squelches accessibility to the conversation. Or so claims Rawls.

As Smith notes, Rawls's claims are simplistic. Martin Luther King, Jr. and Abraham Joshua Heschel appealed to overtly religious reasons to support civil rights without ending the conversation in any way. Furthermore, if we bracket our comprehensive commitments, it turns out we have very little of substance to say on matters of importance. Enforced secularity, enforced neutrality, leaves us with "nothing very probing or substantial to say," and "looks like a recipe for a discourse that is assured in advance of being shallow, empty, and pointless."[9] Also, there are no principled reasons to exclude religion or other comprehensive accounts from the discussion to begin with, and this kind of liberalism or secularity simply presupposes its own truth while imposing it on everyone. Obeying Rawls capitulates to secular rationality for no reason whatsoever, and, furthermore, secular rationality is not remotely neutral but smuggles its own comprehensive commitments through the "rules" of the conversation. As Cardinal Scola once argued, this kind of

---

[9] Ibid., 218–19.

secularity is not neutral but equates "secular" with "non-religious," and thus "the public square becomes predisposed to harmonize itself with all the different visions and practices except those of religion."[10] Neutrality is hardly neutral but smuggles in irreligiosity and trains citizens to treat religion as either ignorant bias or something too meaningless to matter. Tails I win, heads you lose, and you must agree to the coin flip per the rules of the game. To add insult to injury, after making the discussion shallow and pointless, the same theorists precluding religion then complain about depoliticization and disengagement from discourse.

Against all this, a genuine politics is one for humans as we are, aptly described by Voegelin:

> Man is not a self-created, autonomous being carrying the origin and meaning of his existence within himself. He is not a divine *causa sui*; from the experience of his life in precarious existence within the limits of birth and death there rather arises the wondering question about the ultimate ground, the *aitia* or *prote arche*, of all reality and specifically his own. The question is inherent in the experience from which it rises; the *zoon noun echon* [the living being that possesses Nous] that experiences itself as a living being is at the same time conscious of the questionable character attaching to this status. Man, when he experiences himself as existent, discovers his specific humanity as that of the questioner. . . .[11]

If we forget the full range of questions, we lose ourselves.

---

[10] Cardinal Angelo Scola, *Let's Not Forget God: Freedom of Faith, Culture, and Politics* (New York: Image, 2014), 81.
[11] "Reason: The Classic Experience," 92.

## *Negative Frenzy*

In consequence of these factors, we observe a frenzy of activism in our time, although we are still coming to terms with the *activism of negation*. In the next chapter I'll explore the "constructive" sense of activism, which coheres fairly well with modernity's sense of being unleashed, finally, to make the world as humans want it to be. If there is a God who has created the world in keeping with His goodness and good purpose, the good life must include some sense of living in keeping with nature, and that the world and humans have some intrinsic limits or structures that are to be discovered, recognized, and honored, even obeyed. If there is no God, and the world is merely force open to our prediction and control through counter-force, the Baconian project of reason serving to better the human lot makes sense. So, too, politics needn't be understood as soulcraft whereby laws and other institutions exist to help individuals live in keeping with reason and attain the fulfillment of their given natures in keeping with natural law, but can be a more expansive dream of changing the world. Until now philosophy attempted to understand the world, until now science hoped to grasp causes, but now we shall make the world as we would have it—the dreams of Bacon, Marx, Comte, and many others. This vision has a long pedigree and we're quite accustomed to it, even if it is sometimes exhausting and a source of its own anxious frenzy. That's for the next chapter.

What we have not yet thoroughly grasped, I suggest, or even if we have grasped have not yet lived through to emerge on the other side into sanity, is the frenzied activism of negation. The older humanists, if one wishes to call them that, in their way wished to better man's estate by ending famine, disease, war, scarcity, poverty, inequality, and injustice through advances in technology, education, politics, economics, and social harmony. As many scholars have noted, such a constructive vision could be thought of as a secularized eschatology, an attempt to bring heaven to earth, the human effort to make the kingdom of God in the here and now. It was an immanentized eschaton, but it was essentially a constructive project, for better or worse. The new frenzy is an activism not of construction but of negation.

A secularized eschatology still maintained, perhaps unwittingly, some sense of normativity and human nature—it suffered from a theological hangover, it was haunted by Christianity's claims. Once, however, human nature is denuded, and humanitarianism has no content to it, no nature, no reality, the point is to undo, to liberate and emancipate. At least for several decades now, perhaps longer (I won't quibble), many of the most prominent movements in the West have had no constructive vision other than emancipation. It's easy to understand what they wish to be liberated *from*—religion, morals, encumbrances, limits— but it's not at all obvious what they wish to be liberated *for*, what would ever satisfy their frenzy. They do not seem to build towards anything or for anything, but rather to undo and take apart.

Perhaps the clearest example of this is the sexual revolution. Already in the 1920s Wilhelm Reich was urging an unmaking of monogamy, family, sexual mores, restrictions, all of which he viewed as repressive and the main cause of unhappiness, aggression, and violence in the world. If only we could undo any sense of teleology in sex, what he called a finalistic view, repression would end and freedom reign. He never said these words, but he would have supported the spirit of 1968—*Il est interdit d'interdire*, it is forbidden to forbid—and we observe the same impetus in all those thinkers hoping to undo repression and the fixity of sexual norms, language, law, and religion.[12] Anti-authoritarian, to be sure, and purportedly resulting in the maximization of happiness, but happiness is defined negatively as whatever occurs in the absence of repression. Happiness has no content; if there were content, it would be authoritarian, thereby repressive, and thus not happiness. As Augusto Del Noce aptly says, this vision removes all trace of an "order of ends" or "meta-empirical authority of values." This vision has no dialogue or compromise with classical metaphysics and a story of being, goodness, and truth.

Things must be critiqued and taken apart, unmasked and unveiled, so there can be an undifferentiated, undefined freedom, although once even morality is critiqued there becomes no real reason to support emancipation, for it cannot be seen to have a substantive goodness or content. Instead, all that remains is a frenzy of negation, removing all vestige of norm and purpose, and as long as any vestiges remain, so too does the frenzy of activism. Just now, the frenzy is directed against the body. It might be thought odd that the sexual revolution, supposedly about the freedom of the body, has as its condition of possibility first the *in*fertility of the body, then the *termination* of pregnancy, and now turns its fury against the sexed body itself, and we observe the mutilation and amputation of the body, puberty blockers, and so on. I don't know what will happen next, but

---

[12] For a helpful discussion of Reich and others, see Augusto Del Noce, "The Ascendance of Eroticism," in *The Crisis of Modernity*, trans. Carlo Lancellotti (Montreal & Kingston, ON: McGill-Queen's University Press, 2014), 157–88.

transgenderism might be the apotheosis of negative frenzy in the name of contentless freedom.

The energy behind these negations will not dissipate, for they do not seek anything. They will never come to rest in an actualized, finalized state of accomplishment—they seek to actualize nothing, they have no terminus or resting point. One could multiply references to theorists and thinkers, but perhaps Jacques Derrida's "messianicity without messianism" is sufficient, where he hopes not for a messiah or a messianic age, for that would have content, structure, and fixity and thus be monstrous, but excludes all content, asking for unceasing, endless deconstruction, which is freedom. This hope is for the "im-possible," that which has no "horizon of expectation . . . *telos*, formation, form, or teleological pre-formation."[13]

This is, quite simply, hopefulness without hope, a hopefulness that we will have freedom just so long as we have no real content or structure about which to hope. This is negative frenzy.

[13] Jacques Derrida, *Rogues: Two Essays on Reason*, trans. Pascale-Anne Brault and Michael Naas (Stanford, CA: Stanford University Press, 2005), 144.

# 5

## Fever Dreams of Rationalism

GIVEN THE STATE OF THINGS, the temptation to suc-
cumb to moral panic is understandable. It would be easy to
conclude that both our *culture* and our *civilization* are wob-
bling, with culture understood as a set of judgments of
value and civilization indicating the systems of economy
and infrastructure.[1] Our culture has long promoted sexual
revolution, abortion, gender ideology, family collapse, religious indifferentism, ideological conformity, transgender
contagion, and a seemingly endless litany of confusion and
decadence. Now, additionally, cities and states fail to maintain public safety and health while roads crater, bridges sag,
electric grids fail, wildfires burn out of control, and the
water supply is either tainted or disappearing. Culture has
long seemed moribund, now civilization teeters as well.

It's understandable that calls for patience, moderation, or
hopefulness might appear unresponsive, even ridiculous;
when the ship is capsizing, lifeboats are needed rather more
than another symposium. Even so, panic doesn't get life-

---

[1] Earlier versions of parts of this chapter have appeared in *Public Dis-
course*: "The Truth of Sensible Politics" (May 15, 2023); "Don't Panic"
(August 30, 2022); "Lost in the Chaos: The Danger of Total Politics"
(August 19, 2021); "How Should Conservatives Respond to Revolution?"
(April 4, 2023).

boats safely away. In light of the prevalent mood of urgency, I've come to appreciate the thought of Michael Oakeshott, often returning to his collection *Rationalism in Politics*.[2] Particularly insightful is his commentary on a character type, the rationalist, suffering "a deep distrust of time, an impatient hunger for eternity and an irritable nervousness in the face of everything topical and transitory." Rationalists look for perfection, for problems to be solved, for uniform order, and want these immediately and completely. Incompleteness and shoddiness offend them, and they demand the placidity and stability of eternity even now. Rationalists, unlike the activists of negation, attempt a construction, thinking it possible to create a version of heaven on earth. They look to the future, trying to fast-forward to that desirable state.

Non-rationalists, like me, don't look for perfection in the human realm—certainly not in politics—acknowledging the crooked timber of humanity. Finitude and freedom are the very conditions of the humane and the decent, even if the risk of freedom's misuse accompanies these conditions. We are human—*too* human, sometimes—and fallen, but our well-being is thwarted if order comes at freedom's expense. We cannot be free without the real possibility of ignorance, confusion, mistake, and wickedness. To be a person is always to risk acting badly, but the human person is created for his own sake; order is for persons, not persons for order.

I offer no ode to freedom as such. I, like many others, tire of those who wink at or defend the grotesque, the indecent,

---

[2] Michael Oakeshott, *Rationalism in Politics and Other Essays* (Indianapolis: Liberty Fund, 1991), 5–42.

or the immoral in the name of a misguided freedom. I recoil at the so-called "blessings of liberty" when those "blessings" degrade souls and maim bodies. I'm a moral realist, affirming that moral truths exist and can be known. Thus better and worse ways of acting, reasonable and unreasonable societies, and virtuous and vicious persons also exist. Authentic liberty is a freedom for excellence, the capacity and disposition to act well, to do as we ought, not merely as we will. Autonomy is not a good *per se*.

Yet the law alone cannot make us good; only acting persons, through their choices, make themselves evil or good. Deranged law and social norms can fail to educate individuals in choosing well, yet the person becomes good or evil *only* by means of his free act. There is no other possibility for creatures such as we are, persons—no matter how maddening, how frustrating, how exasperating that fact. Thus, the Second Vatican Council maintains a truth known by both revelation and reason, and which cannot be otherwise, namely:

> It is in accordance with their dignity as persons—that is, beings endowed with reason and free will and therefore privileged to bear personal responsibility— that all men should be at once impelled by nature and also bound by a moral obligation to seek the truth, especially religious truth. . . . However, men cannot discharge these obligations in a manner in keeping with their own nature unless they enjoy immunity from external coercion as well as psychological freedom.[3]

[3] Vatican II, *Dignitatis humanae* (December 7, 1965), 2.

## *Idyllic Rationalism*

The term "rationalist" is perhaps confusing, suggesting Descartes or Spinoza or a particular theory of knowledge or metaphysics, whereas Oakeshott intends something broader. He identifies a tenor of mind and character, one disposed to need certainty and fixity but bothered or irritated by impermanence, change, incompleteness, and time. Such a character has a rage for order and cannot but suffer an anxious repulsion at disorder. Even the partially ordered outrages them for its impurity. Oakeshott correctly observes the ubiquity of rationalism on both the left and the right, for it "has come to color the ideas, not merely of one, but of all political persuasions, and to flow over every party line." In one way, the rationalist looks much like a caricature of the Enlightenment, committed to reason understood as "the *enemy* of authority, of prejudice, of the merely traditional, customary or habitual," and thus skeptical of much. Skepticism is coupled with optimism, however, "because the Rationalist never doubts the power of his 'reason' (when properly applied) to determine the worth of a thing, the truth of an opinion or the propriety of an action." Rationalists affirm that reason is held in common by all humans, but finds it "difficult to believe that anyone who can think . . . will think differently from himself."

In the history of ideas the rationalist is often described as committed to axiomatic and deductive reason, which isn't quite adequate, Oakeshott suggests; better to say that he has little regard for the accumulation of experience within a culture or tradition until and unless it is turned into a formula or technique. Committed to viewing the intellect as a tool, rationalists have "none of that *negative capability*" of "accepting the mysteries and uncertainties of experience," and do not give an impression of being the heirs of an education "designed to initiate them into the tradition and achievements of their civilization." Instead, they have a "well-trained" intellect, a tool highly polished and tuned for analysis, programs, and projects, but hardly at all for the accumulation of wisdom and the political prudence needed for dealing with humans as they actually are.

Of all human endeavors, politics might be considered the most resistant to rationalism, since it is in the domain of contingent action, deliberation, freedom, compromise, the transitory, and uncertainty. Euclidean geometry fits the rationalist mold, quite unlike wrangling votes from people with competing motivations, commitments, and interests—there are no necessary axioms in politics, only proverbs. Maybe so, says Oakeshott, and yet the temper and mood of the rationalist is evident whenever "political activity consists in bringing the social, political, legal and institutional inheritance of his society before the tribunal of his intellect; and the rest is rational administration, 'reason' exercising . . . jurisdiction over the circumstances of the case."

The late Roger Scruton insisted that conservatism was always about inheritance, a "*settlement*" binding people "to the place, the customs, the history and the people that are theirs."[4] Politics begins with a sense of "belonging," of membership in a particular people and its ways, including respect and gratitude for the accomplishments of this particular way. Not so the rationalist, says Oakeshott, who sees

---

[4] Roger Scruton, *Conservatism: An Invitation to the Great Tradition* (New York: All Points Books, 2017), 1–7.

no reason to value something merely because it existed for generations: "familiarity has no worth, and nothing is to be left standing for want of scrutiny." Destruction and creation come far more naturally to this disposition than does reform or patching up. Good enough is not good enough for the rationalist, and instead of gratitude for the good attained by custom, he "puts something of his own making"—the rationalist *has a plan*, always modeled on the dispositions of the engineer rather than the elder.

A supposedly rational solution has no patience for the "best under the circumstances" and instead alters circumstances to fit perfection in every detail. As a result of perfectionism, a politics of "uniformity" is sought: "a scheme which does not recognize circumstance can have no place for variety." There must be the *best* form of government, the *only* rational solution, and therefore a perfect and universal political arrangement; allowing "any relevant part of the society to escape from the solution is . . . to countenance irrationality." Quite obviously rationalism in politics is ideological, a (false) commitment to attaining "more certain knowledge about man and society" than is possible. Reality itself bows before the "sovereignty of technique." If only we follow technique, we will solve the human predicament, once and for all, and things shall be as they should be, as they could be, as they *will* be once rational mastery is exercised over human affairs.

This is an idyll, and a vicious one: an utter fabrication, an impossibility, and a dangerous threat to human well-being and agency. Still, it is alive and well, on both left and right. Wokeness, for instance, is a type of rationalism, since any deviation from its orthodoxy must be ripped out root and branch, leaving no dissent or hesitation to fester and corrupt. The impure, the unbeliever, the heterodox, even the hesitant are all thought contagious, a threat to be eradicated. At the same time, the right, long non-rationalistic in orientation, now suspects Scruton's conservatism is devoted to a world no longer existing, if it ever did. Rather than "ordered liberty," the terms which young conservatives think better describe reality include the following: carnage, emergency, crisis, depravity, degradation, decadence, collapse, and illegitimacy. Many suggest it is time to reject civility, neutrality, free speech, originalism, fusionism, separation of Church and state, liberalism, right-liberalism, little platoons, and localism. Instead of Plato, Aquinas, Madison, and Jefferson, we ought (apparently) to read Donoso Cortes, Julius Evola, Ernst Jünger, and Carl Schmitt. (If those names are unfamiliar, trust me when I say they are familiar to young, restless conservatives of the moment.)

The young conservative observes not order, but disorder: drugs, deaths of despair, tent camps, fatherlessness, the lowest rates of marriage ever, non-replacement levels of birthrates, ubiquitous pornography (and of the most violent and vulgar sort), corrupt and rotten institutions, failed education systems, pointless (but utterly expensive) colleges and universities, crushing student-loan debt and inability to purchase a house, gig economies, rust belt towns, miserably incompetent elites, the collapse of religion, the absence of marriageable men, endless war, national debt, and open borders and open markets. We are no longer the yeoman farmers of Jefferson or the commercial republicans of Hamilton but an unhealthy, enervated, exhausted, alienated, numbed populace zoned out on the filth produced by our anti-culture. Only the blind, the foolish, think otherwise. This mood, while perhaps understandable, is conservative rationalism, a mood of rejection of inheritance, a mood of irritation looking for something far better than what is on offer; and, indeed, the right is awash in new schools, new plans, new programs, and plans to fix things, to solve our problems and *now*.

Conservatism has fractured into many stories, each vying tremendously with each other. Big ideas are being embraced or repudiated, and there is *much* passion about it all. It makes sense that this is so. Things do seem to have fallen apart, the center does seem wobbly, and some older conservative institutions and policies are non-responsive to current needs. This is natural: when many, especially many of the young, feel the status quo is failing, new theories and positions will emerge, each attempting to reframe the story, capture imaginations, and win arguments and votes. This is to be expected, even welcomed. Fences need to be painted from time to time so they don't rot; conservatives shouldn't refuse to paint out of some strange nostalgia for the status quo. Conservatives are not ideologues but inclined to cautious empiricism in politics, embracing what is sensible, workable, moral and decent, but without demanding perfection or stasis. If what we've been doing and thinking no longer responds, the genuine conservative does something better. The creation of a decent society never stops, and didn't stop in 1776, 1989, or 2015.

With schools and camps arguing and competing, times like ours can be exciting, or exasperating, or enraging. That, too, is perfectly normal, and can even end up being a source of new life, energy, alliances, and policies if we manage to avoid tearing ourselves to shreds. I, for one, mostly welcome it, although I do wish we could dispute arguments rather than persons—but *ad hominem* is also to be expected. Conservatives realize we live in a time of revolution, of wildness, and as the revolution continues its monstrous but endless destruction our own responses will be incomplete and even confused. Conservatives don't long nostalgically for a world no longer existing, but attempt to live in ordered liberty, find the truth of being, realize the common good, and embrace a disposition of joy, gratitude, and delight.

However, the plans are usually ideological visions of technique. The administrative state will fix things; Rome will fix things; the common good will fix things; a new Aristotelian elite will fix things; a better nationalism will fix things, etc., etc. Whether we like it or not, we are left with people as they are: free and yet still responsible for searching for the truth and live in harmony with the truth as they understand it, and responsible for properly forming their intellect and conscience to appropriately exercise that freedom. But freedom it remains, even when performed miserably—inattentively, unintelligently, unreasonably, and irresponsibly. We are left with people as they happen to be, which can be disappointing, to say the least. Of course, law helps train conscience and choice, but law cannot replace choice and maintain moral agency.

Just now, there is too much panic. Too many indulge their fear of contagion, their purity tests; too many have given themselves over to a hatred of the human condition and wish we were gods outside of time and change, ignorance and conversion, repentance and forgiveness.

We remain just what we are: dependent rational animals, limited creatures within space and time, prone to error and confusion. But this reality, this impoverishment, is the condition of our freedom, our *being human*. Panic, irritation, and reluctance to forgive reveal a distaste for humanity; it betrays what Walker Percy called "angelism." I see this as a pathology of mind or spirit, and it is has infected the left and right, liberal and conservative, believer and unbeliever.

## *Total Politics*

Politics-as-ultimate seems evident everywhere. Obviously, there's endless hectoring or lecturing in social settings, as everyone must share his or her expertise, but that's more bad manners than a harm. More disturbing is the impulse, on both left and right, to want politics to be overly involved and ambitious, to want power to solve the human condition, to have the state push thick goals, to overcome the limits and burdens of very human challenges. It's all destined to fail, because it's simply beyond the competence of government, and it's all too dangerous, with the state absorbing enormous swaths of what ought to be left for civic associations and families. Every human lives out the drama of existence in his or her way, and with great risk: they gain or lose heaven, embrace or reject love, bring a child into being or not, form friendships and romances or sink into loneliness, become sages or fools. Every life is a fascinating mystery of agency and conscience, virtue and vice, and that drama can be played out successfully even under the conditions of imperfection. We don't need politics to absorb all, and we would be well advised to keep the fully human things in their place of primacy, and politics confined within prudent limits and modest aims. If we forget or forgo the primacy of the person, choosing instead the story of power and chaos, it seems likely we'll lose the cosmos of our own souls.

There is wisdom in Plato's *Republic* where just after constructing the best city in speech, including plans for sharing of spouses, children raised almost entirely by the city, eugenics, and a rigid class system, he winks and calls into question how literally we are to take the idea of a perfect city in the first place.[5] In Book V, Socrates notes, somewhat defensively, that the exercises in "constructing the good city" have been "for the sake of a pattern," a model in thought, but not at all about "proving that it's possible" to bring such a city into actual existence. "Don't compel me," he says, "to present it as coming into being in every way in deed as we described in speech," since it is "the nature of acting to attain to less truth than speaking."

As we all know, a theory of politics is not so difficult to formulate—likely we all have one, imagining that if only we were able to rule all would be well, all manner of things should be well. Perhaps we grudgingly admit that since we're constrained by the current system not all of our reforms would work, but it would be a pretty good city, far better than the current regime, if our ideas were followed. Let's call this "rule by late-night dorm-room discussion." Every college sophomore interested in politics has created a utopian system; now *if only* it could be implemented. Alas, a good many professors of political theory believe the same.

Plato, though, is stating rather more than the obvious fact that it is difficult to implement theories. He does *not* say, "some details of our city in speech will need to be moderated to pass Congress or pass Constitutional scrutiny." Instead, his claim is more interesting, revealing an understanding of political reason, albeit an imperfect one bettered by Aristotle: "it is the nature of acting to attain to less

---

[5] Plato, *The Republic of Plato*, trans. Allan Bloom (New York: Basic Books, 1968).

truth than speaking." On this reading, Plato indicates a scant interest in applied politics. He never seriously proposed bringing the city of speech into reality, even in a limited or truncated form; instead, the project was always a defense of philosophy as a higher form of life. Action, and perhaps especially political action, is never as true as philosophy. For those who seek truth, thus, the political life recedes in interest while philosophy ascends.

Aristotle understands the problem better than does his teacher. In the *Nicomachean Ethics* he notes that the well-schooled person knows the type and limits of precision admitted by each sort of discipline and human endeavor: one does not ask for probability from geometry or certainty from rhetoric.[6] (This, incidentally, is why Aristotle suggests the young are not ready for politics, lacking, as they do, the experience needed to be well-schooled—consider late-night dorm-room sessions.) In ethics, as in politics, "the end aimed at is not knowledge but action."

To distinguish knowledge from action is *not* to distinguish *truth* from action. Plato might think truth is not in action, but Aristotle makes no such mistake. There certainly *is* truth to be found in action, but it is the truth of action and not the truth of theory. Aristotle knows reality is variegated, of more than one type, and so too reason and truth exist in more than one form. For instance, some aspects of reality not created by us or dependent upon us are known by us through various forms of theory. These would include the natural sciences, philosophy, theology, and so on. There is also the knowledge of thought itself, including the ability to order thought. This is logic. A third

[6] Aristotle, *Nicomachean Ethics*, I.3, 1094b23–30.

form of knowledge produces and makes—*techne* and poetry. Another type is found in action, the domain of ethics and politics. Science, logic, *techne*, and ethics are not reducible to each other, nor are the truths of each reducible to each other, and yet none is untrue or *less* true for that. Instead, they are true in their own proper and fitting way. Ethics demands practical reason—prudence—while logic does not.

Not only is the truth of action to be found through prudence—understanding the right time, right way, right means, right extent—but prudence does so in concrete and particular circumstances. Some actions are always morally wrong, Aristotle says: there is no right way or right time to commit adultery. Right action, on the other hand, is always what *this* person in *this* moment with *these* particular circumstances should do. Certainly there are helpful generalities known through tradition and law and custom and proverb, but still, it is *you,* and only *you*, who must act *here* and *now* in *these* circumstances. Consequently, Voegelin rightly notes, there is "in concrete action a higher degree of truth than [in] general principles of ethics."[7] The specifics have "more truth, for in action we are dealing with concrete things."

Again, this does *not* mean that specifics have more truth than generalities or than theory just as such; not at all. Instead, the specifics contain more truth with respect to action. In metaphysics the generalities have more truth than this or that experience or emotional response about the world, because metaphysics is the articulation of universal principles of being. One would not ask a metaphysi-

[7] Voegelin, *Anamnesis,* 148.

cian about particular experiences of being, but for an account of the principles of all real things; in action we are not looking for universal principles of all real things, but for what the correct action is here and now by this person in this situation. (This is not relativism or perspectivism or situationism, by the way, for there really is a truth of the concrete act, and that truth cannot allow for what is immoral or vicious.) In ethics and politics, thus, there is more truth to be found in the concrete specifics of particular actions than in the city of speech. Plato got it only partly right, although he began a chain of reflection allowing us to understand this political insight.

Not just *a* political insight but perhaps *the* political insight: politics has its own proper form of reason, and it is reason concerning what is good and possible to do, given the political specifics of a particular people at a particular time and with their form of government. Not only is this not a theoretical abstraction, it is opposed to theoretical abstractions; not only is this not about late-night dorm-room utopias, it is opposed to such as dangerous nonsense.

Actual politics is not "Settlers of Catan" world-making, nor an exercise of fiat and theorizing. In politics we remember (and those who forget are dangerous) moral limits, limits to coercion, our limited knowledge, and the limits of our prudential powers. We can know moral truth, and we can know the truth of a political action—what to do and when—but it is far more difficult to know the truth of action than it is to know the truth of theory. This seems counterintuitive to some, but it is more difficult to be a statesman than to be a physicist. Or, certainly there are far more competent physicists than there have ever been competent statesmen. I'm not suggesting a winking cynicism about the possibility of moral rights and wrongs, but political sensibility is not found in imaginary utopias, dreams of perfection, or big, brash theories of politics, but in the actual details of human action.

The political warriors of our time are not well-schooled. They have forgotten (if they ever knew) the nature of political and ethical truth, and they go to war with the wrong weapons. They will discover that theory and rationalism and artificial visions of the cosmic common good are entirely unsuited to the task and demands at hand. On the other hand, while "sensible, adult politics" might not get the blood stirring as a slogan, it is in fact the place and home of the wise.

## Frozen Intellects

Briefly, I want to hint at a variant of the idyll of rationalism, namely, the disappointed rationalist, or fundamentalist. I do not mean this in the religious sense, precisely, as in the fundamentalist Christian or Islamic fundamentalist, although historically the emergence of religious fundamentalism has some relation to the intellectual disposition I mean. Fundamentalism in its Christian guise arrived fairly recently, in the late 19th century, as a response to theological liberalism, although a response of a certain type. John Henry Newman also responded to theological liberalism, and didn't hesitate to affirm the dogmatic truths of the Church; but consider the suppleness of mind exhibited by Newman. He rejects theological liberalism, he accepts the authority of the Church, but his move to Rome came after significant scholarship on the history of doctrine and a conclusion that doctrine develops. Of course, Newman has a quite specific sense of development, which rejects random innovations, let alone contradictions or reversals of the deposit of faith; still, a doctrine defined by the Church long after the founding of the Church can be a genuine development rather than a distortion or error.[8] Protestant fundamentalism, on the contrary, rightly viewed liberalism with alarm, correctly insisted that certain key doctrines could not be explained away by the modernists without greatly distorting the Christian claim, but also tended—perhaps not necessarily, but a tendency—to literalism, theological primitivism (if it was early it is true, if it is later it is not true, contra Newman), and eventually, in America at least, to anti-intellectualism and a suspicion of science. (It's much more complicated than this, but these tendencies are noticeable.)

I'm not here interested in religious fundamentalism in itself, but rather what this too-brief description reveals about a certain cast of mind, namely, a tendency to attempt to freeze thought, to fix it, to stop development. If rationalism in its pure form looks to the future, to bringing the eschaton to the present through our schemes and techniques, fundamentalism, often in a disappointed exhaustion, looks to the past, to a time when things were ordered and healthy. Like the rationalist, the fundamentalist views the current state with skepticism, as unacceptable and in need of complete repair; as with rationalism, a reform or a patch is deemed a kind of treason; as with rationalism, the solution is universal and need not respond to circumstances; as with rationalism, the solution has a kind of ultimacy. Once fixed, always fixed, that is to say, frozen. The

---

[8] John Henry Newman, *An Essay on Development of Christian Doctrine* (South Bend, IN: University of Notre Dame Press, 1994).

fundamentalist, as a type of rationalist, wants time to stop, wishes our politics to have a kind of eternity, but an eternity of what once was.

## *Habits of Hope*

The antidote to despair is not perfect politics, an impossibility, a mere ideology; the cure is *hope*. Moral panic reveals despair at the state of things: craving the fullness of the kingdom of heaven *now*, but upon discovering decadence and depravity—and who can deny our time's troubles—responding with the sadness of despair. Despair cannot be overcome with certainty or perfection, but only by hope and the truth of concrete action undertaken in the light of hope.

For the rationalist or fundamentalist character, hope cannot but seem inadequate, even silly. The world is in flames and I suggest hope—how quaint. But hope is not blind, or merely optimistic, nor is hope something we churn up in ourselves as a kind of subjective attitude. Hope is a virtue. It is a state that perfects us, makes us well, capable of thinking, living, and acting in the freedom of excellence, as flourishing human beings.

As we will explore in the final chapter, Benedict XVI suggests that hope has become reduced to its "subjective sense, as an expression of an interior attitude," a "disposition of the subject," rather than a genuine virtue. Virtues bring an affective training and expression with them, of course, but they are never reduced to a temperament or an attitude. Reducing hope to an airy atmosphere makes it somewhat disreputable, a kind of silliness. As a virtue, however, hope is a perfection of human intellect, will, and disposition, an ability to live a fully human life in keeping with our flourishing and full well-being. To lack hope is to lack humanity, to be incomplete in the training of our personhood.

It is a common temptation to attempt to replace virtue with a hack of some sort. Immoderate in appetite? Try this diet pill. Unfriendly and impersonal? Here's a book on how to win friends. Without hope in this world? Not a problem; here's some program of political or social action that is *guaranteed* to make things well. And if that program fails, we have a back-up plan. Of course, when such plans invariably fail to overcome the human condition, excuses are made— "*if only* we had more money," or "*if only* the Founders had written differently." Or the counsels of despair kick in, hacks are abandoned, and we conclude, "there's nothing to be done." As a result, we see an oscillating cycle of extravagantly optimistic plans coupled with counsels of despair and panic. Hope avoids both, knowing full well that the human condition will never be resolved through politics and, still, that we remain agents capable of acting with intelligence to improve the commonwealth.

Ordinary action moves from experience, to intelligence, to judgment, to choice; hope is the sort of virtue that starts at the end of that list and governs the lower from the higher, so to speak. That is, the person of hope will make choices in keeping with hope (rather than despair), and judgments will be in keeping with sound choice, intelligence in keeping with sound judgment, and experience formed by intelligence. The higher governs and directs the lower. For those oscillating between optimistic plans and despair, on the other hand, the higher also governs the lower, albeit in a mode bereft of virtue and thus distorted and irrational.

All the virtues are needed at all times, but hope is perhaps especially needed in our own. Politics is not first; phi-

97

losophy is prior, and even that is servant to theology. Reversing the order is a drastic mistake, albeit an all-but-inevitable error for those lost in chaos. When the universe is utterly immanent, when the human is reduced, when culture is simply entertainment, it is hardly surprising that politics will occupy the center of thought and imagination. Such a politics thinks too highly of itself. Not only does a politics of ultimacy attempt to govern the entirety or *totality* of human affairs, it also exhibits a *finality* or completeness in its judgments. If there is a transcendent reality beyond human control, politics isn't *total*—doesn't include everything—for politics is simply incompetent in some domains of human life. If there is a divine authority, the judgments of politics are not *final*, for they are subordinate to the judgments of God. In our own moment, politics seems all-encompassing, inserting its snout into what is properly private, personal, or associational, and political judgments seem to be of considerable importance, tantamount to the demanding claims of morality.

Just now, however, politics seems to be the only game in town—everything is political!—and absolutist, dogmatic, and accompanied by an aura of hyperventilating moralism. Somewhat counter-intuitively, the more we are lost in the chaos, with the human reduced to mere matter and chemicals, and where God is dead, the more fervent and demanding politics becomes, even though reductionism lacks any capacity to ground or justify any moral or political norms. A thoroughgoing reductionism cannot *in any way* justify human dignity, or equality, or justice, for such things simply do not mean anything in a universe in which everything is merely matter in motion. As it turns out, the old fear that religion was a conversation-stopper and resulted in political dogmatism overlooked the more worrisome culprit: the (incoherent) dogmatism of immanentized secularism.

# 6

## Enchanting Sirens

FOR SOME, NO PREDICAMENT EXISTS. Simply embrace enchantment, they suggest. This is easier said than done since it is all but impossible to wind the clock back to the pre-modern worldview. Modern science explains things better than its progenitors, albeit with flattening tendencies. Dante claimed that Aristotle was the master of those who know, which might still be the case, but Aristotle was incorrect when claiming rocks fell because seeking their proper place in the universe—gravity is a better explanation. If we are to avoid self-deception and maintain intellectual probity we should admit that the immanent frame is the starting point, even if we keep an open-world system. We're modern people existing in modern conditions of belief.

Given modern malaise, it's unsurprising to observe an outpouring of books about re-enchantment but not many about enchantment pure and simple. These are different concepts. A French peasant of the thirteenth century lived under conditions of belief in which enchantment was the way things were, and she didn't need to concoct anything, nor did she feel conspicuous in her sense of powers and forces in the world. She wasn't buffered or immanentized; we are. A project of re-enchantment, then, is not a simple return to the time of enchantment unencumbered with the knowledge and conditions of belief of our own age. This changes things. To take an example, there are various movements of neo-traditionalism, but this is not the same as tradition as such. (I am not criticizing, merely observing.) If one lives and moves and has one's being within a thick and lively tradition one doesn't tend to think of it as a tradition—it's just the way things are, the way things are done. It's reality, not chosen but inhabited. It is the horizon of meaning and clears the way for living. Neo-traditionalism, on the other hand, cannot avoid self-consciousness, quite aware, sometimes painfully so, that it is chosen, that things could be different and are different for most other people. Neo-traditionalism always grapples with genealogy; it knows its own origin story unobscured by the mists of time and lacking a venerable ancestry. "Neo-" implies that something was lost and recovered, but if recovered, optional, chosen, revived, and if chosen and revived then perhaps invented and concocted. Is this real?

Also, if we return, do others think we are pretending? As Taylor recognizes, re-enchanters cannot help looking over their shoulders to see if others notice what they are doing. If others are not embracing re-enchantment it makes the enchanters conspicuous. They stand out, and the question lurks in their own mind: have I become that college friend who took Tolkien too seriously and bought the replica swords and taught himself Elvish? It's embarrassing. The problem, put starkly: every attempt to re-enchant the world is experienced with more self-consciousness than was present in the original enchanted world. It cannot be otherwise. Again, I am not criticizing individuals; the problem is inherent to the program.

## *The Break*

In 1952 the British poet David Jones published his epic poem *The Anathemata*, a lengthy and complex retelling of the history and symbols of Britain, all with reference to the Mass.[1] Jones attempts to revivify the symbols of Britain, to make them alive so there might again exist the *anathemata*, things set apart, so that cultural signs might mean again and poetry regain its force. The poem is complicated, but his explanation is not. As a poet he deals in signs, but signs must work. If a sign no longer signifies it cannot function as a medium—but it turns out that in a disenchanted age poetry might be invalid:

> The artist deals wholly in signs. His signs must be valid, that is valid for him and, normally, for the culture that has made him. But there is a time factor affecting these signs. If a requisite now-ness is not present, the sign, valid in itself, is apt to suffer a kind of invalidation.[2]

Consequently, he wonders if "the kind of thing I have been trying to make is no longer makeable in the kind of way in which I have tried to make it," if it would be no more than an "absurd affectation" to pretend that this was not a genuine possibility.

According to Jones, by the 1920s his artistic circles had identified "The Break," indicating some point when "Western Man moved across a rubicon" and the old symbols no longer functioned in art or religion. He does not question

[1] David Jones, *The Anathemata: Fragments of an Attempted Writing* (London: Faber and Faber, 1952).
[2] Ibid., 15.

the truth of his Catholic religion or its dogmas, all of which he affirms, since "our speculations . . . were upon how increasingly isolated such dogma had become, owing to the turn civilization had taken, affecting signs in general and the whole notion and concept of signs," including the sacraments. The teaching about the sacraments is true, and yet there has been a "lesion" in historical memory which makes the culture forgetful and not apt to understand them.

For a contemporary reference, consider Tara Isabella Burton's vivid descriptions of sophisticated young New Yorkers flirting with the "weird" parts of Christianity.[3] During COVID, she reports, many of her cohort zoomed in to traditional expressions of worship such as Gregorian chant, compline, and the Latin Mass. (She attends an Episcopal parish.) Quarantine pushed some people to take religion more seriously, and many were drawn to "particular expressions . . . with their anachronistic language and sense of historical pageantry." Young people, particularly those "disillusioned by the political binaries" and "the crisis of modernity and the liberal-capitalist faith in individualism," are "finding solace in a decidedly anti-modern vision of faith," since "old forms of religiosity offer a glimpse of the transcendent beyond the present." This is Weird Christianity, rejecting not only watery mainline denominations but also "Republican Party politics" and the crises of presentism.

Despite these experiments, almost none of her cohort are traditionally religious at heart, and many "might get a sense of communal identity from CrossFit, say, or meditate or read tarot cards to get in touch with a sense of the transcen-

---

[3] Tara Isabella Burton, "Christianity Gets Weird," *New York Times* (May 8, 2020).

dent." Her weird acquaintances practice an amalgam of traditionalism and punk—it's a kind of rebelliousness. Interestingly, while she notes a desire for faith claims that are "totally demanding" rather than accommodating to the culture, it's also the case that, like punk, Weird Christianity has and is an aesthetic, a preference for "Elizabethan-era language" or the "wearing of veils." An aesthetic—she quotes Rod Dreher—of attraction to "aesthetic forms of Christian worship."

In a later essay, Julia Yost explored a similar phenomenon, again highlighting the rebellious streak among young adults in "'Dimes Square,' a downtown Manhattan neighborhood popular with a pandemic-weary Generation Z—or Zoomer —crowd. . . . Its sensibility is more transgressive than progressive . . . whether sincerely or as fashionable statement."[4] Among the cultural products—ironical or not— are "Trump hats and 'tradwife' frocks, monarchist and antifeminist sentiments," with Catholicism acting as the "ultimate expression of this contrarian aesthetic." The mood indicates wry tiredness at progressivism's stranglehold, and in such a context Catholicism is hyper-subversive, although it's unclear "whether the new faithful are performing an act of theater or not. . . ." One of the people discussed, an actress on a hit television show, is a revert once known for her socialism but now describing herself as "Catholic, like Andy Warhol."

Several of those interviewed by Yost admit their faith is "a pose," a role-play, but since "that's what religion is," in the words of one, faith in the "absence of perfect belief"—cer-

---

[4] Julia Yost, "New York's Hottest Club Is the Catholic Church," *New York Times* (August 9, 2022).

tainly faith without dogma—is as real as anything else in the world of simulacra and stimulation. Not just this cultural moment, either, Yost notes, recalling the Decadent movement of Oscar Wilde, when converting was a way to escape the confines of English Protestantism. In fact, Yost states, the word "pervert" historically meant someone who went popish.

Given Catholicism's supposed transgressive nature, the Met's 2018 exhibition *Heavenly Bodies* cheerfully placed religious icons alongside sado-masochistic "paraphernalia." Naturally, some Catholics objected to the show, but for those wishing to violate current mores, "for reasons substantive or stylistic," such "affectation of religious imagery and faith" allows symbolic resistance against social orthodoxy.

Burton understands that all this might be posing, an exercise in faux-authenticity. In another essay Burton describes a time when she observed traditional gender and sex roles and "started wearing mostly skirts" because her fiancé desired it.[5] Here she cautions against concluding that if something is premodern or nostalgic or offensive to the current mood it is "automatically good, because it is both ancient and transgressive." There is "a danger" in fetishizing "a nostalgia for the Medieval era." But as she and Yost both see it, the central impulse of Weird Christianity is reacting against the current mood; it just is a fetishization of the weird past against the boring present.

Furthermore, authentic tradition isn't well-suited to picking and choosing the parts you like and ignoring the other

[5] Tara Isabella Burton, "Bad Traditionalism," *Commonweal* (July 6, 2020).

bits. What is the principled standard for putting on and taking off aspects of a tradition the way one might change clothing styles? It's hard to avoid the conclusion that Weird Christianity is an externalization of selfhood, the consumption of a ready-made identity that attained meaning before "the Break" but is now a safe fantasy providing an image of selfhood without substance—or substantial burdens. This uses religion as an avatar, a public presentation of a self that *looks like* the selfhood one's great-grandmother *really* had, but which remains cosplay for the residents of Dimes Square. As fantasy, it allows one to play at something real, but safely, without the demands and obligations experienced by those who actually belong to a thick tradition and its many encumbrances. Great-grandma was a real self, but she wasn't conducting experiments in living, and her tradition placed heavy obligations on her. Fantasy from a great distance is LARPing, like an American tourist dressing in the academic regalia of Hogwarts, a pretend school mimicking Oxford, with Oxford itself "a place from which the spirit has fled, leaving the towers and spires where they are, still a heartbreaking, uplifting sight from the surrounding hills in any light, but hardly anyone still knows what they mean and why there are there."[6] Such attempts at re-enchantment are circles of self-referentiality, bereft of the substance that once made the real things real—and everyone knows it. It's a pop culture remix of old classics.

It's difficult to know when you are making a fetish of something, or merely constructing an aesthetic mood, or posturing; or simply having an affectation, or picking and choosing traditions. All attempts to re-enchant run smack

[6] Peter Hitchens, "Alice's Oxford," *First Things* (November 10, 2017).

into this problem, or will in the presence of any self-aware-ness. Enchantment was easy; re-enchantment is hard to do without embarrassing yourself.

## *Safe Fantasy*

From one perspective, re-enchantment should be easy. After all, we're aware that disenchantment was intentional, the result of choice, but hardly necessitated by the nature of reality itself. Therefore, can't we simply chose otherwise and go back to the way it was? The sociologist Philip Rieff once noted that "culture is the form of fighting before the firing actually begins. . . . [Cultural] work is the matter and man-ner of disarming competing cultures."[7] That is to say, every culture works to sustain itself and to disarm competitors, and its weapons are the principles of legitimization and del-egitimization, what is thought acceptable and what is ruled out of bounds, impossible for "right-thinking people" to hold or believe or value. That is fighting before the firing begins. If our current culture resulted from a fight, not from reality itself, there's no principled reason to not fight back and walk ourselves back to enchantment. Or so it seems to some.

According to Rieff, we are nearing the end of a great cul-tural fight, a momentous struggle of legitimization and del-egitimization. He distinguishes between first, second, and third cultures. First cultures are typically pagan and enchanted, often with multiple gods and a thin or perme-able barrier between the divine and mundane orders. Order

---

[7] Philip Rieff, *My Life among the Deathworks: Illustrations of the Aes-thetics of Authority* (Charlottesville: University of Virginia Press, 2006), 1–30.

is sacred, policed by taboos. Second cultures are generally derived from purportedly revealed monotheism. Sacred order is governed by a self-revealed creator, and the world is sacred, but it is faith rather than fate, and providence rather than magic, that shows God's active role in history. Natural law is at home in this second world. Consider Benedict XVI's Regensburg Address, in which he argues that the synthesis of Hellenism and Biblical faith lead to the conclusion that "not to act in accordance with reason is contrary to God's nature." God is *logos*, and all that He wills is reasonable; He cannot will that which is unreasonable, and He communicates this reasonableness to us in various ways, including our own reason, which is the source of human law. Just human law, on this account, is reasonable, and human reason participates in the eternal law of God.

While second culture limps on in the vestiges of our common life through the waning presence and influence of Judeo-Christian institutions and norms, it is, thinks Rieff, *relentlessly* being swept away in the fires of a great cultural fight, with third culture emerging victorious. Third culture does not posit a sacred order; instead, it is radically skeptical of any such claims, so skeptical that its defining characteristic is the negation of second culture. It is a negative culture, destructive, an undoing; Rieff calls it *anti-culture*. Like every culture, third culture is interested in maintaining its own way and delegitimizing other ways, and our current skeptical anti-culture is relentless in sweeping away, critiquing, and unmasking the authority of second culture. We see this, for instance, in the suspicion towards traditional marriage, sexual strictures, and cultural norms, and in the rejection of an intrinsic relation of sex to gender. The current masters of suspicion, our guiding elites, are "virtuosi of de-creation," and they are consumed with a passion to delegitimize sacred texts, reason, and moral inheritance. Our third culture wishes to be emancipated from traditional order.

If we undid a culture, perhaps intentionally, why can't we just wind it back, re-enchant it? If the medieval person inhabited a universe with the music of the orbs making the very cosmos sing, can we not simply sing (*cantare*, the root of enchant) again? Or, as Alan Jacobs asks, might it not be possible to keep the benefits of the buffered self's immunity to demons and threats while keeping the porous self's openness to "white magic" and meaning?[8] Can't we return to the best bits of first and second cultures without the nasty stuff, the way Weird Christians keep the cool bits of Catholic externals without all the challenging moral teaching? Not quite, he suggests, although the desire to do so explains the rise and popularity of fantasy as a genre, whereby the modern self "strives to avail itself of the unpredictable excitements of the porous self while retaining its protective buffers." It is a "*safe* simulacrum of the pre-modern porous self." A simulacrum, however, isn't the real thing. Fantasies are stories *about* enchanted worlds, not artifacts *of* enchanted worlds. They are enchant*ing* to us, but they are not themselves enchant*ed*.

It's notable that the attempts to re-enchant take place after Judaism and Christianity—second cultures—already emptied the world of some of its charge and porousness. Of course these religions maintain the existence of a transcendent God and His ability to work within the world, but

---

[8] Alan Jacobs, "Fantasy and the Buffered Self," *The New Atlantis* (Winter 2014).

already the very first words of Genesis proclaim that there are not other gods, and the usual options—sun, moon, stars, trees, rivers, and seas—are impotent and derivative. Or consider the confrontation of Elijah and the priests of Baal (1 Kings 18) in which both pray for their competing deities to set the sacrifice aflame. The priests of Baal pray and cry and cut themselves with swords, accompanied by the mockery of Elijah suggesting that perhaps Baal was asleep or on a journey. No one answered except the God of Elijah. Something similar happens with St Patrick and the pagan feast of "Baal's fire" in the Ireland of 433.

Whatever their differences, Jews and Christians share a horror of idolatry and unmask idols as rocks and wood, and such things cannot be God; Jews and Christians empty the world of some of its charge and some of its porousness. Not entirely, of course, but significantly. They concentrate charge into the agency of the one true God and His acts. Catholics and the Orthodox maintain a heightened sense of charge but the "white magic" is specified and ordered, requiring certain people to act *in persona Christi* and only in those things Christ ordained and established and allowed. Magic is focused and magicians are deputized rather than possessing their own force. The Reformers go further: all is given over to the providence and act of God. But the world has been drained of much of its spiritual energy, as Jacobs puts it, by Christianity itself, and the world of science and technology awaits to administer the *coup de grâce*. We're not going back to a world where fairy stories are believed.

Enchantment stories are just that—stories—for the modern person. Tolkien certainly thought that fantasy revealed something true about the world and humans within it, but he was joking when he said hobbits still exist but are careful not to be seen. Fantasy allows us to experience something of the delight and horror experienced by our medieval ancestors, but we experience it safely ensconced in our chair with the central heat on, and terror contained within the pages of the book or the flickering of the screen we can close if the experience turns frightening—no Paschal candles needed. We know this, and when we read about young Wiccans or druids at Stonehenge, or the revival of Norse religion, we can't help but sigh and feel slightly embarrassed for these people. They've forgotten it's not real, or they've play-acted for so long as to sink into their characters. Attending a fantasy convention dressed as an elf is embarrassing; thinking you are an elf is illness.

Jacobs remarks on the power of the digital world to augment and replace the actual world, and thus to grant people a *sense* of power and transcendence again. The online fantasy allows one to enter hyper-reality, more real, dynamic, alive, and enchanting than the real world. Online you can fly, hurl fireballs, fight dragons, encounter demons… things are charged! But, of course, things are not charged: we simply have an experience as if they were, and we know the difference. This is all simulacra and fiction, code, and electrons. It is not enchanted but enchanting, by which I mean that it can be experienced as bewitching or intoxicating, and give something of the experience available to an earlier age. However, that something enchants *us* does not mean it is itself enchanted. It lacks that substance; it does not have being; it is not charged in itself and cannot act on us, even if we sing ourselves into a state. And it all ends when unplugged, and thin, immanent reality sets in again. It is fantasy, and we know this.

## *Very Much in the World*

In no way do I intend a critique of tradition; I'm a proponent of tradition understood rationally, embrace the tradition of the Church as authoritative, and consider tradition a source of wisdom and a corrective to the pretensions of rationalism. Neither am I criticizing the fantasy genre or liturgical renewal or Gregorian chant or Latin—these are not what I have in mind as faux-enchantments or enchanting idylls. I'm thinking of four main categories of enchanting sirens, which I'll only briefly detail. All these function like Olga's reinforced door; they promise a kind of security against the threats and dangers of the world, but in the end, once they fail, and they cannot but fail, they trap people within immanence dramatically and completely.

First, soft and hard varieties of neo-paganism. By hard neo-paganism I mean ongoing and increasingly prevalent attempts to recover old-school paganism, although with modern additions, including witchcraft and druids, modern Norse and Germanic paganism, esoteric gnostic spiritualities, and that vague constellation of positive thinking, alternative medicine, and chakra, well described as "woo woo."[9] Soft-paganism, which I take to be less objectionable but mostly ridiculous, includes the make-believe world—but not *entirely* make-believe, for self-identification is often intensely caught up in these practices—of the cult of body modification, cosplaying, Comic Con, and similar practices. I'd also include the growing phenomenon of neo-

[9] For examples, see Molly Hanson, "Could Neo-paganism Be the New 'Religion' of America?," *Big Think* (Sept. 30, 2019); Mark Peters, "The Norse Gods' Unlikely Comeback," *Boston Globe* (Nov. 4, 2017); "Commitment (The Woo Woo Issue)," *Los Angeles Times* (Aug. 2022).

Nietzschean vitalism in the very-online world of Bronze Age Pervert and his ilk.[10] These variations of paganism all want some sort of escape from the numbness of contemporary western life but without the strictures of the Judeo-Christian options, and generally return to pre-Christian or non-western options. This includes a bewildering range, from upscale yoga studios, to taking anime too seriously, to actual belief in the Norse gods, to a pre-Socratic sense of stylized warrior culture. All are idylls.

Second, aestheticized, weird Christianity. For all I know, turning to Anglo-Catholicism, Orthodoxy, or Roman Catholicism in a performative aesthetic experiment to escape the insufferable tyranny and utter tedium of a West fashioned in the image of John Rawls, Oxfam, Judith Butler, and the *New York Times* may serve as *praeambula fidei*—preambles of faith—in the way that Aristotle's philosophy cleared the ground for dogmatic theology. I hope so, and I do not protest anyone trying to find meaning and search for the truth through beauty. Ratzinger somewhere noted that the main sources of evangelization which remain today are beauty and the holiness of the saints. John the Baptist likely would have been at home with the people of Dimes Square, and beauty really can call us beyond ourselves to God. At the same time, there are some obligations required in belief, practice, and conduct that go beyond a ritualized performance of non-conformity. Weird Christianity might be a halfway house to the real thing, but to stay in aesthetical religiosity is to embrace an idyll.

Third, versions of mainstream Christianity that for rea-

[10] Graeme Wood, "How Bronze Age Pervert Charmed the Far Right," *The Atlantic* (September 2023).

113

sons of literary taste, or a certain mood of *Sehnsucht*, or to capture a certain pose or stance towards the world, embrace the vision of the sacramental imagination without believing in the actual sacraments. I have high regard for C. S. Lewis and Tolkien, but there is a tendency, even a kind of danger, of reading them and then affirming that the world is broadly sacramental—avoiding "the Break"—while denying the reality, meaning, and efficacy of baptism or the Eucharist. This is an idyll, as nicely identified by Matthew Schmitz:

> There's a lot of talk about how Catholics have something called the "sacramental imagination." Often this is said sentimentally, as if Catholics were romantic savages who view everything as suffused with wonderment and beauty, enchanted people who climb up and down the rungs of the analogy of being. This is a way of talking around the actual content of the faith. What the sacramental imagination should mean, first of all, is actual belief in the sacraments: Marriage is indissoluble and ordained by God. Christ is present in the Eucharist and must be revered. My grandparents in their concern for my baptism were much better examples of the sacramental imagination than all the faith-in-fiction litterateurs combined. The sacrament of baptism was real to them, and so long as I went without it, they feared my damnation. They had the sacramental imagination in that cold, narrow sense. My parents did not.[11]

---

[11] Julia Yost and Matthew Schmitz, "A Conversation between Two Converts," *First Things* (November 12, 2018). A slightly longer version of that interview can be found in R. J. Snell and Robert P. George, *Mind, Heart, and Soul: Intellectuals and the Path to Rome* (Charlotte: TAN Books, 2018).

Obviously there are varying theologies about the sacraments, and I'm not suggesting one is idyllic unless holding the Roman Catholic view of the sacraments, a view I affirm as true. At the same time, if one denies the notion, meaning, history, and efficacy of *the* sacraments, positing meaning and efficacy in the sacramental imagination is a safe fantasy, a literary pose, and it signifies absolutely nothing. Christianity is not a variant of romanticism, and while there is much romance in the Faith, you cannot have the romance without the *res*, without the real. All too many people are actively working to create a fiction of enchantment, pretending dragons are real and the world is haunted all while insisting that the things actually charged by God remain merely symbolic and empty. You can't have the wardrobe without the tabernacle, however, or your imagination is empty invention rather than an access to the real. (Flannery O'Connor might still have said it best: if the Eucharist is only a symbol, to hell with it.)

Fourth, political fantasies. I've already discussed the idylls of activism and rationalism, but I return to political fantasy here as well, in part because of its prevalence at the moment. There is a lot of chatter, much of it palliative fantasy motivated by honest frustration at the nonsense of contemporary politics. I understand and resonate with the frustration, but returning to monarchy, reestablishing the papal states, waiting for a new Christendom, establishing theonomy, and granting special governing privileges to the elect, while *perhaps* making for entertaining but unedifying dorm room debates, are not serious political options in the United States. To take them seriously is to be politically unserious, to flee into a fantastical realm of the unreal where things are better, safer, and ordered. In fact, I suspect that a whole lot of engagement in politics is a kind of idyll in a politics-as-entertainment or political-rage-as-redemptive mode.

Opposed to these four enchanting sirens is the non-fantastical, non-idyllic vocation of Christian disciples, who are very much at home among the mundane ordinary things of the world. In the Gospels we certainly read of miracles, and a miracle occurs every day at every altar in parishes the world over, and still these miracles tend to be about ordinary things. Sometimes the dead are raised and demons cast out, but Our Lord also heals a blind man, an ill woman, a feverish child. The apostles fish, mend nets, collect bread, have dinner, visit their friends and family, go to weddings, bicker, and spend a lot of time walking. The most significant event in history—the Christ event—mostly looked like everyone else's life. "Isn't this the carpenter, the carpenter's son?" ask the people of Nazareth, since Jesus didn't seem much different than the other residents of that insignificant town (Mt 13:55). Even the sacraments—those miracles of salvation—begin as the most ordinary of things in the world: water, bread, wine, oil, hands, words, bodies.

In describing the Knight of Faith, Kierkegaard notes that he's unremarkable, indistinguishable from anyone else. True, sometimes weird and amazing things happen, but not usually, and we're never instructed to hope for them, let alone view them as salvific. True religion cares for widows and orphans, true religion keeps the prayers, the teaching, and ordinary life together. The apostles weren't especially unusual people, not remarkably accomplished people, not amazingly talented people, and neither are the disciples of our moment, us.

To be a Christian is to be very much in the world, and in

the world as it is. I do not mean we accommodate the world's errors or affirm its wickedness—*compossessores mundi, non erroris*, possessors of the world but not its errors, says Tertullian—merely that the stage upon which our salvation and the salvation of all occurs is the very world we now inhabit, with all its non-fantastical ways. It's quotidian. And yet, in that ordinariness, the ordinariness of everyday life, the drama of our souls and the acts of God bring all things to fulfillment.

As we know all too well, that drama is sometimes a slog. Not at all idyllic. Full of tedium and labor, suffering and worry, bills and squabbles, failures and disappointments, pain and sadness. Also joys and loves, delight and laughter, merriment and marriage, children and grandchildren, gardens and baseball. The drama of salvation is mostly ordinary joys and ordinary woes, ordinary tasks and ordinary accomplishments, and still the most important things—the kingdom of heaven, friendship with God, our final destiny—saturate the mundane. To flee the ordinary for fantasy, to flee the mundane for the enchanting, misses the point, neglects our responsibility, and denies our vocation as sons and daughters of God. We're very much at home in the world, and we ought to be.

I've examined the malaises of the moment and the idylls of temptation. I turn now to hope, although first sketching a metaphysics and cognitional theory robust enough, I think, to give hope a place to take up residence, but forthright and sensible enough to avoid idyllism.

# PART III

## Recovering Hope

# 7

# A Generative World

MY HESITATION about enchanting by literary fiat is not to deny the plenitude of being or accept a stingy universe, as deftly articulated in the ontology of Thomas Aquinas. I'm against romanticism without the *res*, but there is a *res*; reality has a structure, and it is in fact good. Aquinas's early work *De ente et essentia* is often read as an exercise in dry scholastic logic, but underlying the dryness is a metaphysics of dynamic, saturated creation, where immanence abounds with the outpoured goodness of transcendence.[1] His metaphysics, without any hint of fantasy or preciousness, depicts reality as generous and dynamic, avoiding malaise or idyll. *De ente* is highly technical and I won't work through every detail, but I suggest that in addition to its precise logic an ontology is expressed. Ontology is the branch of metaphysics accounting for being (onto-logy); here I present an account of being rooted in the logic of Aquinas but emphasizing the dynamism and energy present in it. With Aquinas we begin with logic, but his mind is not dusty and fusty—there is something *exciting* going on in this text, something lively and energetic. Scholastics sometimes forget that the Aquinas of syllogism is the same man who

---

[1] Thomas Aquinas, *De ente et essentia*, trans. Robert T. Miller (Medieval Sourcebook: Fordham University, 1997).

wrote Eucharistic hymns. He is not a thinker to be treated reductively.

## *Being, Essence, Matter*

Being and essence are the first objects of the mind, Aquinas states, for we have no concepts without drawing upon a sense of being. "Cat" comes to mind more readily than "being" for a child, but to point at or think "cat" is already to suppose "the cat *is*…" or "that *is* a cat," however implicitly. Still, sound analysis begins with what is first for us, and Aquinas starts with being before proceeding to essence, since essence recognizes something more differentiated and designated than being, namely, *what* a thing is. Not just "there is something" but "there is a *cat*, and a cat is a feline."

Essence is "that through which a thing is constituted" in "its proper genus or species"—quiddity or whatness—and what is signified or intended to be known by a definition, since definition articulates the genus and specific difference of a thing. Humans belong to the genus animal but with the specific difference of rationality, like the other animals but with a root capacity for reason. A definition articulates the essence of the thing while essence constitutes the thing as "a particular kind of thing," a *this* rather than a *that*, and *of this sort.*

Unlike substance dualists who affirm two distinct entities, a soul and a body, Thomas follows Aristotle's hylomorphic account. Things are different with angels and God, but every embodied material thing is one substance, just one thing, with two principles, form and matter, both equally necessary for the substance to be and to be intelligible. (For living entities we say soul and body rather than form and matter, but that's only to acknowledge animation.) Now, which is the essence—form or matter? Platonists say form, because form is the cause of the thing's whatness, its being the sort of the thing it is, and matter has no intelligibility of its own without being in-formed. When we know something, we know what is intelligible about it, the form. Materialists choose matter, for they don't believe in the existence of form except as the arrangement of matter, but it is the arrangement of matter which exists and is knowable. For Thomas, both are incorrect.

Matter is not a principle of cognition or intelligibility. Matter is a passive principle only intelligible when informed and en-acted, and it is form which is the principle of intelligibility and act. Form causes the intelligibility of matter, but form alone is not essence. When we define any physical substance, the definition always refers, and cannot but refer, to the matter of a thing. Humans are rational *animals*, and not disembodied loci of reason. Triangles are three-sided figures with three angles totaling 180 degrees. Without sides and figure, it's not a triangle. So it is "that the term essence, used with respect to composite substances, signifies that which is composed of matter and form." Composite substances are composite, after all, and thus cannot have essence as either matter *or* form, but always refers to matter *and* form.

Here's where things get tricky. The Thomist has no hesitation affirming the existence of universals. Every human being has the very same essence, for all are rational animals. Every triangle shares the same essence, for all are triangles whether equilateral or scalene. Furthermore, these essences are not conventions or names given to things for convenience, and Thomas affirms the existence of universals, albeit not in a Platonic sense where universals exist independently of intellect and matter. Matter, though, is not universal; matter is the principle of individuation. If all humans have the same intelligibility, and that intelligibility is real, not merely concocted, then Socrates would not be distinguishable from Plato except that their bodies make them distinct individuals. Socrates and Plato are specifically identical—they have an identical essence—but are numerically distinct because of their bodies. All triangles have the same essential properties, but we have triangles in many textbooks, and also triangles of different sorts, because of the individuation of this wooden piece, this bit of plastic, these lines on this page or chalkboard.

If matter is always particular, and essence is always with reference to matter, it does not seem possible to affirm the universality of the essence. Or perhaps Socrates and Plato have distinct matter but aren't equivalent to their own essence, instead participating in an essence distinct from them—Platonism. It looks like we have to choose either nominalism, denying universals, or Platonism, denying that entities have and are their own essence. Aquinas skirts this by distinguishing designated and non-designated matter, or signate and in-signate.

Hylomorphism views essence as involving both matter and form, not either alone, but does not depict essence with reference to any particular body. Every triangle will be a three-sided figure with interior angles equaling 180 degrees, thus both form and matter, but the matter referred to in the definition indicates no specific triangle. This particular triangle is a toy made of red wood; that one is yellow and plastic; this one is a black line in a textbook; that one is chalk on a chalkboard in this room in a middle school. That is, any actually existing triangles will be made of some matter arranged in these properties. The definition indicates that triangles will have these formal properties of necessity *and* that any actual triangles will be material in some way, but the definition does not refer to wood or red or plastic or chalk, all of which are particular significations.

Similarly, the human being is a composite of soul and body, for the human is a rational animal. All humans are essentially rational... and also essentially embodied. (Recall that we confess the resurrection of the body and not the immortality of the soul in the Creed, and that if Christ did not actually rise from the dead with a body then Christianity isn't true.) Humans are embodied, essentially so, but the definition of "human" makes no reference to the particular designated matter of my body or your body or his body or her body—just that the human will have *a* body. My body is designated matter; it is this body, this unity of matter in this time and place operating in systematic function. Your body is different designated matter; it is that unity of matter in that time and place operating in another systematic function. Essence refers only to non-signate or non-designated matter. It says there will be a body of a rational animal type, but it leaves undesignated the particular arrangement of muscle and bone: "I call signate matter matter considered under determinate dimensions. Signate matter is not included in the definition of man as man, but signate matter would be included in the definition of Socrates if Socrates had a definition." In reality, the essence of Socrates and the essence of human differ only in that the human as such has non-designated matter, which entails that Socrates have designated matter. But the essence is the same.

## *A Hospitable World*

Essence refers to both form and non-designated matter, while an actual body (signate matter) is informed by form and individuated by matter to be this particular human, Socrates or Plato. However, signate matter is already suggested or implied by non-designated; designation is implicit, contained within the idea of non-designation so that the intelligibility is hospitable to, disposed to, and awaiting designation. The one concept is friendly to the other. Let me explain what I mean by this with some additional points from *De ente et essentia*.

Immediately after making the distinction between non-designated/designated matter, Thomas uses it as the basis of an analogy with genus/species. "Similarly," he claims, "the essence of a genus and the essence of a species differ as signate from non-signate, although . . . a different mode of designation is used with respect to both." The individual is matter determined by dimensions—this particular length, width, and height—while the species is determined not by dimensions but by specific or "constitutive difference," although the determination "is not through something that exists in the essence of the species but in no way exists in the essence of the genus." That is, non-signate matter has no dimensions, but becomes determined by designated dimensions not hostile to or imposed on the intelligibility contained already by non-designate matter. Non-designated matter's intelligibility is open to, and already refers to, designation, even though it does not possess designation itself. Similarly, the determinations that make the species different than the genus (rational rather than only animal) are "also in the genus as undetermined." Animal is not merely a "part of man," for then it could not be predicated of us essentially, but animal is "all that man is," meaning man is essentially and entirely animal, although with a rational perfection. The genus already contains the perfections of the species implicitly, is not resistant or alien to something true of the species; species is not something foreign to the genus but is instead a further determination *of* the genus. The genus *has* the perfection of the species implicit within it, and it is natural to the genus for it to be specified in this additional way. The genus "awaits" further development and perfection.

Aquinas provides the example of how the term "body" might be understood. If we think of body as the genus of animal, so that the more general category of body could be particularized as an animal body (as distinct from an inanimate body), then it follows that body is not a property that happens to be joined to animal but already contains animal within it in an undetermined way. He explains: if we think the term "body" signifies "designability in three dimensions and nothing more," then there is no further perfection or specification that can follow from it. That is, if body simply means "three-dimensionality," full stop, with the term "body" having exhausted or completed its meaning with reference to dimensionality, then the term "animal body" is a conjoining or linking of two entirely distinct concepts, animal and body. Animal means a living thing, body means three dimensions, but animal is "superadded," in Thomas's language, to body with no intrinsic relation between the two terms. Body means dimensionality and no more—it is complete and exhausted by that description.

On the other hand, body could be understood as signifying a thing that will have three dimensions *and* that from this some further perfection could proceed. If the genus body is understood in this fashion, then the term "animal" does not need to have "body" conjoined to it, for animal already implies body since animal is a particular specification or type of body. Body would thus be the genuine genus of animal and there would be "understood in animal nothing that is not implicitly contained in body."

Let's take a more simple example. Consider the genus shape. Circles, triangles, squares, and hexagons are all shapes. Is it the case that when we define a circle—a set of coplanar points equidistant from a central point—we need to then also say, as a sort of tack-on, something not already understood, "oh, yes, and that set of coplanar points also happens to be a shape"? That seems wrong. Isn't it rather the case that we already knew the circle to be an instance of a shape and so don't include or add the word "shape" to the definition because circle is already known as a shape and it would be redundant to add the word? The category of shape, as a genus, already has circle "implicitly contained" within the genus, although circle and triangle and hexagon are distinct instantiations or perfections of the genus shape.

Aquinas goes further. Not only does the genus implicitly contain the species, but the species implicitly contains the individuals. So the genus body contains animality, and animality implicitly contains rational, as in rational animal, and rational animal contains (in a non-designated way) this or that rational animal. Let's use the shape example, which I think easier to grasp: shape implicitly contains triangle, and triangle implicitly contains scalene and right-angled and equilateral and acute and obtuse. Equilateral contains this red, wooden triangular children's toy and that image in a geometry textbook—all, of course, in an indeterminate, non-designated way.

In *De ente* this is all described in terms of the logic of genus and species and individual. We ought not, however much the word "contain" might encourage us to do so, *imagine* a genus as a space in which there are invisible shapes waiting to appear. "Contain" should not be thought of in the sense of a receptacle, but in the sense of meaning. The point is not to imagine the species somehow emerging from the genus or the individual emerging from the species the way a large blob of mercury allows for a smaller bit to squelch out and become a smaller blob of the same stuff while distinct from the "mother blob." Not at all.

Aquinas's point has to do with how essence works within the theory of hylomorphism, where entities are composites. If one is a nominalist, the individual human Socrates either lacks an essence or has his own unique essence not shared with that of Plato. Plato either lacks an essence or has his own unique essence utterly different from that of Socrates. One of them can be human, but not both. Nominalism is incorrect, though. For Thomas, Plato and Socrates both are essentially human, and that essence is a universal they both have (and are) in precisely the same way and with precisely the same meaning. Both are of the essence "rational animal" because that essence indicates individual bodies or particular instantiations of that essence only in a non-designated way, with the designation and particular perfection (or completion) already implied within the broader category. All human beings will be rational animals with bodies, although Plato will have his body and Socrates another.

## What Is Going On? A Comparative Reading

I may have tried your patience these last pages, and perhaps you thought "exactly so" at the words "What is going on?"

—I'll try to explain why I think this matters and is relevant to disenchantment. First, though, I'll give a comparative reading of Genesis 1 to provide a more literary and less uptight sense of what is going on—to illustrate the meaning, not to make an equivalence or claim that Aquinas was trying to justify or prove the truth of Genesis 1 or any such thing.

In the beginning the earth was without form and void—*inanis et vacua*—and the Spirit moved over the face of the waters. Then God acts, through speech—speech that accomplishes and enacts. The categories of genus and species are categories of grammar and logic, and grammar and logic are not trapped within the mind but refer to and relate to the world as it is—in this case, the grammar of God's speech creates the form and content of the world.

There is an order to this creative speech corresponding to the need for form and content, to avoid *inanis et vacua*. God first establishes form, usually described as a separation, in days one through three, and then provides content to those forms on days four through six. For instance, on the first day darkness and light are separated from each other; the second day sees waters separated from waters, resulting in skies and seas; on day three waters are gathered together, allowing dry land to be distinguished from the seas. There is an oddity or uniqueness in the ordering, since day three adds content as well as form: the earth has vegetation to populate it, while all other forms—light, sky, and sea—remain empty, *vacua*, on the day of their making. This is odd not only for breaking the pattern where the other forms remain empty, but also because, as Genesis 2 explicitly says, on the day God made the earth and the heavens there was as yet no plant or herb of the field.

The pattern snaps back on day four, however, where the form—the genus—of light is given content, is specified, with sun, moon, and stars, thereby continuing to separate and distinguish the light from the darkness and also seasons, days, and years. Day five adds content to the form of day two, with the waters now bringing forth "swarms of living creatures" and birds to fill the sky. All, as is repeated multiple times, "according to their kind"—according to their essence (Gen 1:20–21). The sixth day brings more entities, each in its own kind, and the living creatures to fill the earth come forth. And as is quite fitting, it is on the same day that God breathes his image and likeness into existence: the rational animal is made on the same day as the other animals—not on a later day, as if the human is not essentially animal. We are animals, and the entirety of the genus animal is true and applies to our essence, even though our essence refers also to a particular perfection of animality, i.e., rationality. We are entirely animal; we are entirely rational. These are not distinct parts or radically distinct forms somehow conjoined, as would be implied if created on different days. Yet animals have a distinct break from vegetation, hurried into existence on day three, even prior to the sun needed for their sustenance.

While compact and without Aristotelian categories of logic and metaphysics, Genesis 1 is remarkably similar in its implications to *De ente et essentia*. Days one to three provide a kind of form or structure—very much like genus—allowing for difference or separation not only between the genera but also between the various species or content within them. For instance, light (as genus) is quite distinct from its privation, darkness, but light has an essence awaiting further perfection or specification, the lights, as well as the distinction between the various lights which are particularized or designated as instances of lights: sun, moon, and stars. Darkness has no essence at all and thus can receive no further perfection or specification, while sun, moon, and stars all belong to the species of "lights" and the genus of "Light."

I'm not claiming Genesis 1 attempts a Thomistic articulation, or that every aspect fits the analysis. This is mainly to give a more literary and approachable illustration of what Thomas is doing. But it does tell us something quite interesting about day six. We have dry land, earth, which is a body, and contains elements (carbon, hydrogen). Animals are perfections of the genus body, and animals are also defined essentially with reference to non-signate matter, including a lot of carbon. Humans are particular perfections of the genus body, are also defined essentially with respect to non-signate matter, including a lot of carbon, and are perfections or completions of the type animal—on the same day (within the same form, same genus) as the animals. Finally, the separation or distinction of male and female follows the very same pattern: the human kind is specified by separation, a distinct completion or perfection or designation of the type, with both male and female essentially human, both essentially rational animals. (The language follows the same pattern. "God created man [species] in his own image . . . male and female [particular perfection] he created them." Also, the individuals Adam and Eve are designated instances of male and female. The pattern fits.)

## Who Cares? A Dynamic World

Perhaps the discussion of Genesis helped make sense of my interpretation of *De ente*, but another question likely remains—who cares? So what? I answer: Aquinas (and Genesis 1) provide a dynamic view of world-process capable of dealing with modern science without losing a vision of intelligibility and essence so often shuttled off by the modern understanding, and without enchanting fantasy. Turns out, old-school metaphysics is nuanced and lively.

In an earlier chapter I discussed the blow modern science lands to the biblical view of the world. Not creation but nature, and not nature so much as universe. Not a good creation but merely a universe of force and motion. Not a good creator known by the goodness of the world. The human as the inventor of the idea of a goodness limited to instrumental purposes and desires rather than a real teleology—and human desires essentially self-serving and fearful. I've also mentioned the problem of historicism: that concepts and values have meaning only within a particular tradition at a particular time, and don't translate universally across culture or even across times. All this calls into question the biblical and Thomistic accounts.

Let's explore a yet more difficult question or problem, one which Aristotelianism and Thomism do not appear well suited to answer, and which, at least in the popular consciousness, all but dooms them to irrelevance or antiquarian interest. Not only, as Jonas put it, is the world governed by its own processes of constitution, but those processes result only in the state of things as they now are but will not be forever. A world of becoming rather than a world of being, with evolution as an obvious example. Things, it appears, are not created after their own kinds, not with a stable, fixed, and abiding essence, but are entirely in flux, in a state of perpetual development. True, we categorize species in taxonomies, but those are fated to change as evolution continues. The idea of a stable, permanent human nature fixed since the sixth day of creation without substantial change is not viewed as compatible with the best of contemporary science.

Even more, the question of essence is simply irrelevant since the advent of early modern science. Consider the fate of Aristotle's four causes: as he would have it, understanding a thing requires grasping its material, efficient, formal, and final cause. Early modern thinkers such as Francis Bacon, Descartes, Spinoza, and Hobbes unanimously reject this schema and the Scholastics who maintained it. Finality, or teleology, just isn't to be discovered scientifically, they thought, and was irrelevant to understanding how things worked; it was a distraction serving only to deform and slow our understanding. Formal cause was also discarded. Modern science is not especially keen to study the underlying essence of things; rather, the concern is to understand how things relate to other things and to see how things function or work. That is, the interest fundamentally shifts to material and efficient cause, or how to grasp the functions and actions of things, especially to predict and control those functions for our betterment. Essence is irrelevant.

Richard Rorty boasts that the old categories of essence, accident, substance, and property are replaced with "a picture of the flux of continually changing relations."[2] Everything is in a state of becoming as the forces of the universe constitute things in a dynamic and evolutionary way, and since there is no God to speak things into existence "after their kind," there is no place for stable, fixed, static essences,

---

[2] Richard Rorty, "A World without Substances or Essences," in *Philosophy and Social Hope* (New York: Penguin Books, 1999), 47–71, at 47.

which serve no interesting scientific purpose anyway. As he puts it, to know a thing is to "do something with or to" it, and "to put it into relation with something else." Consequently, knowing has nothing to do with "something intrinsic" to that object. There is no "inner core," and "no such thing as a nonrelational feature . . . any more than there is such a thing as the intrinsic nature" or essence of a thing. Knowledge, such as it is, "is defined by antiessentialists not in terms of a relation to intrinsic features of objects. . . ."

On the face of it, the logic of *De ente* seems in antiquarian opposition to these claims, and Rorty suspects we are forced either to double down on anti-modern essentialism or capitulate by abandoning the Thomistic account. Either you apprehend essence through a definition and know what is unchanging, and thus will not have "any exigence for changing forms, structures, methods," or you conceive of things as a "concrete aggregate developing over time."[3] On my reading of the text, this is a false dichotomy, for *De ente* has a kind of dynamism built in, although, again, one has to read it as a dynamic ontology rather than a static grammar.

The genus has further specifications already contained within it in an implicit and indeterminate mode. In one sense this means only that what is true of the essence of the genus is also entirely true of the essence of species, so that the rational animal is essentially animal and the specification doesn't remove the genus from the particular or merely get conjoined. What is true essentially of animal is also essentially true of rational animal, and essentially true of

---

[3] Bernard Lonergan, *A Second Collection* (Toronto: University of Toronto Press, 1974), 1–9, at 5.

Plato and Socrates as well. But let's consider that something more dynamic is at play.

Thomas affirms the following two commitments: (1) the good seeks to communicate itself, and (2) all things seek full act, full perfection. I'll cite two texts, although there are many such as these.

> For natural beings have a natural inclination not only toward their own proper good, to acquire it, if not possessed, and if possessed, to rest therein; but also to diffuse their own goodness among others as far as possible. Hence we see that every agent, insofar as it exists in act and possesses some perfection, produces something similar to itself.[4]

> It follows upon the superabundance proper to perfection as such that the perfection which something has it can communicate to another. Communication follows upon the very intelligibility (*ratio*) of actuality. Hence every form is of itself communicable.[5]

Being in act is intrinsically active and self-communicative. It diffuses itself, it gives itself, and such self-communication "is actually the whole point, the natural perfection or flowering of being itself, the goal of its very presence in the universe," according to Norris Clarke. Clarke insists that the seeking and giving of beings is "one of the central themes in the thought of Aquinas." And let's not forget that God speaks forth—communicates—in creation, even speaking forth his own image and likeness.

---

[4] *Summa Theologica* I. 19. 2, cited in W. Norris Clarke, "Person, Being, and St Thomas," *Communio* 19 (Winter, 1992): 601–18, at 604.
[5] *Summa contra Gentiles*, III. 64, cited in Clarke, at 604.

I interpret *De ente* in such a fashion. Being is not best understood as static essence, as a frozen self-preservation of unity. Rather, in being there is an innate dynamism, a drive to seek perfection and to communicate perfection. Finite being by its very nature moves to perfect itself, and there is no perfection that does not seek to diffuse itself as much as possible. Being is thus intrinsically active and dynamic in seeking perfection and giving the perfection it already has. If the genus has its own perfection, it seeks to communicate that perfection as far as possible, and if the genus implicitly contains the species in a non-designated way, then it implicitly contains that species and seeks to communicate it, to act toward it, to bring it forth.

In this mode of interpretation, the dry grammar of *De ente* can be transposed somewhat. Thomas says, recall, with reference to the genus body, that it can be understood to mean three-dimensionality and no more, or it can be understood to mean this and "that some further perfection can proceed." The genus signifies the species indeterminately, and whatever is in the species is "in" the genus as undetermined, but it is the perfection of the genus to seek this further perfection and to communicate its perfection to the further specification. The genus is fecund and generative, it is disposed to the species, it is hospitable to it, it awaits it. It seeks it out, and does so by seeking itself out and communicating its own perfection to further specifications of perfection, and it seeks to communicate itself wholly and entirely to those specifications. The universe is friendly and dynamic, being is almost eager to speak itself and bring new specifications of perfection into existence. Being is pregnant. As Hopkins notes, each being "deals out" its own inner being in which it dwells, for "*myself* it speaks and spells," but Aquinas says rather more than this.[6] As being speaks itself and deals out its own inner being it seeks to bring forth that perfection in other things as well. The genus speaks itself forth by speaking itself into additional perfection and specification in the various species. Animality awaits as if with eager groaning the arrival of its rational variety.

The world of becoming, of change and evolution, of history and development, is no threat to Thomas. His metaphysics is fundamentally dynamic. Nature is an internal source of motion or change seeking more act, more perfection, more specification, more instances, more, more, more. Of course nature is one of becoming, for act is not frozen, act is active; act *acts*. Being seeks to blossom, it seeks to unfold its latent possibility, and the genus—since it is being in act—seeks to unfold itself in yet more being, the species, and the species seeks to unfold itself in the individuals, and the individuals seek to unfold themselves in friendship, in polity, in reproduction, in culture.[7] This is dynamic and essentially so.

Furthermore, however much this language of generosity and generativity may sound merely metaphorical, it seems to be taken quite literally by Thomas. Etienne Gilson glosses Aquinas's definition of a cause, *causa importat influxum quemdam ad esse causati*, as meaning that "some-

---

[6] Gerard Manley Hopkins, "As Kingfishers Catch Fire" (1877).

[7] I take the term "unfolding" from Thomas Gricoski's book *Being Unfolded: Edith Stein on the Meaning of Being* (Washington, DC: Catholic University of America Press, 2020), 10. He cites Stein's *Finite and Eternal Being*: "Finite being is the unfolding of meaning . . . actual being is the unfolding outward of an essential form, from potency toward act, in time and space."

thing of the being of the cause passes into the being" of the effect.[8] Of course, a cause can give only what it possesses and can be received only in virtue of what the effect is, and since the species is within the genus in a non-determinative way, there is a real and genuine linkage of being allowing the dynamism to act. But the cause is an actual, not merely metaphorical, gift or bestowal of act. And since to be is to act, to be is to give: "The generosity with which goodness gives of itself is, in the case of an intelligible being, a free manifestation of the energy by which that being exists." All of which is to say, the universe is not starkly cold, though neither are we simply claiming an enchanted mood but recognizing a generative principle in reality itself.

No idyll here, but an ontology disposed to perfection, and predisposed to hope.

---

[8] Etienne Gilson, *The Spirit of Medieval Philosophy,* translated by A. H.C. Downes (South Bend, IN: University of Notre Dame Press, 1991), 86, citing Aquinas *Commentary on the* Metaphysics, Book 5.

# 8

# Fecund Intellects

THERE EXISTS AN inverse relationship between the order of being and the order of discovery: the things most knowable in themselves are the last we discover, and the things first discovered are least knowable in themselves. God is most intelligible and the source of all intelligibility, and yet we do not know God's essence, and even in the Beatific Vision God's essence is not fully comprehended, because God is infinite act—whereas we are quite at home and familiar with the world of sense, and long have been, even though the sensible is not intelligible in its material principle but rather in its form, grasped by the intellect rather than by sense. What is known first to us does not explain itself, and what explains everything else is known to us last. Reality is polymorphic, in other words, with depths and richness: reality is not reducible to the sensible, immanent world.

At the same time, there is an isomorphism—sameness of structure—between the order of being and the order of discovery. The real has an intelligibility, and we can know this intelligibility in its various forms. However, since (a) the real is polymorphic and (b) there is an isomorphism between intellect and the real, then it would seem to follow (c) that the intellect itself must be polymorphic, capable of knowing in various ways, corresponding to various types of reality. I think this is true, and take it to be a key insight in avoiding the malaise of scientism without giving in to the idylls of rationalism or faux-enchantment. The real is dynamic and generative, the intellect is fecund and supple, and thus the orders of being and knowing are disposed to a friendly universe of love and hope.

## Bad Science

For those immune to the siren song of the re-enchantment enterprise and firmly within the camp of modern science, it's not obvious that reality or the methods by which realities are known are polymorphic. A few years ago Leon Wieseltier explored the problem, with particular reference to the thought of the noted Harvard scholar Steven Pinker, correctly noting that science is constitutionally unable to determine either the place of science in society or how science relates to other domains and methods of knowing.[1] Such questions are extra-scientific and cannot be known through the normal scientific means: "Science confers no special authority, it confers no authority at all, for the attempt to answer a nonscientific question. It is not for science to say whether science belongs in morality and politics and art. . . . Nor does science confer any license to extend its categories and its methods beyond its own realms. . . ." None of this, it hardly needs to be said, denies science or its methods, although it strongly resists the ideology of scientism, the idea that science and only science provides genuine knowledge.

As Wieseltier describes it, scientism is a kind of imperialism where the methods of science—entirely proper in their

---

[1] Leon Wieseltier, "Crimes against Humanities," *The New Republic* (September 3, 2013).

own domains—are exported whole-cloth to other loci of knowing. In this, the sciences deform those other kinds of knowing, awkwardly distorting them, or discounting them as not real knowledge, as subjective or not worth knowing. Imagine a "scientific explanation of a painting" studying the chemical analysis of the pigments used to make certain colors, or analyzing human vision. Such an attempt cannot but exhibit "intellectual perfunctoriness" by explaining "everything except what most needs explaining" about the painting. Or consider a study of religion with brain scans of people during prayer, investigations of the health and income outcomes of religious people, discussions of the literacy rates of children in a religious community, and so on; all of this might be exceedingly interesting, worthwhile for many reasons, but none even remotely studies religion as religion; the truth of religion is bracketed or ignored as unimportant or impossible. Religion might be socially useful or not, but if religion has aspects beyond the range of scientific inquiry those regions are shunted into oblivion as non-cognitive or emotivist, perhaps edifying, but not something considered as even possibly true.

Not only does this imperialistic tendency deform or devalue entire swathes of human inquiry, including political theory, aesthetics, ethics, and religion, but it deforms science at the same time. Science performs its inquiries beautifully when restricted to its own fields, but it presents a false view and practice when extended beyond its limits. Scientism is bad science, in other words. In a discussion of Newman's *Idea of a University*, Bernard Lonergan suggests that when a discipline falsely attempts to bear the weight of grounding and integrating the entire range of knowledge, an attempt beyond its power (and properly the task of theology), it "mutilates what of itself is an organic whole" and "causes distortion in the remainder in which man endeavors to compensate for the part that has been suppressed."[2] As a result, such secularism, such scientism, "not only leads to ignorance of religion but also mutilates knowledge as a whole and brings about distortion in what remains."

The most basic distinction in methods of knowing is between the world of common sense and the world of theory, a vivid example of which can be read in Augustine's *Confessions*, where he struggles to understand how God could exist as pure spirit. To exist, he thought, as it is very easy to think, is to exist the way a body exists, to exist *as* a body. We all know what we mean by the existence of a body: it is something already-out-there-now. That is, it exists as perceivable already, before we perceive it; it exists visibly outside our mind, or out there; it exists in a kind of simultaneity of presence, now; and this is what we mean by the reality of bodies. If all reality is bodily, then God is either non-existent or bodily (and thus not the God of classical theism). Augustine can't get over what he calls his "corporeal thinking."

We often do this when we imagine God. In so doing, it is all but impossible to avoid smuggling body into the picture. We imagine heaven as "out there" in outer space or hell as "down there" in some vague way, or imagine God as an impressively bearded old man. This pictures God as an entity we could point at or thump with our hand to know He was real, as if the Webb Space Telescope will look deeply enough into space and see God looking back at us. This is the sort of entity the "new atheists" diligently work to refute.

[2] Lonergan, *Second Collection*, 185.

In his *Confessions*, after what feels to the reader a very lengthy struggle, Augustine rapidly has what Bernard Lonergan calls an intellectual conversion.[3] Not a religious conversion, not that he now believes in God and rushes to the baptismal font, but an intellectual conversion whereby he realizes that bodies are real, to be sure, but not all of reality is bodily. God could exist and not be an already-out-there-now version of the real. On Lonergan's reading, Augustine recognizes that the world of common sense—rocks and trees and cars, the world of bodies—has a shape of knowing entirely proper to it but non-transferrable to other domains of the real. When we try to know bodies we certainly begin with data of sensation: smelling, hearing, pointing, seeing, and sometimes thumping, which we then understand before considering if our understanding is adequate and sufficient to the object and the data. However, if we export the conception of reality, the already-out-there-now, and the shape of knowledge of that kind of reality to other areas of our questioning we've committed a significant mistake. Instead, we should realize the range of intelligence is not always attempting to know bodies but to know whatever can be intelligently conceived and rationally affirmed, although never indifferent to sensation, for as Aristotle and Thomas remind us, "there is nothing in the intellect not first in the senses." Natural theology, the knowledge of God available to unaided reason, is a reckoning with the intelligibility of the world and explanations of that intelligibility, including how to make sense of God as the cause of the world, but it is not natural science, even when paying atten-

---

[3] See especially Bernard Lonergan, *Insight: A Study of Human Understanding* (London: Darton, Longman, and Todd, 1973), 245–79.

tion to the results of science; neither is it looking for God as if a body out there in outer space. We are attempting to understand the conditions of intelligibility and the currency of this attempt is the work of understanding, argument, intelligibility, reasons, and explanation. No pointing or thumping involved.

Consequently, Wieseltier is not engaged in special pleading for the humanities when he scoffs at Pinker's handwaving away of "traditional causes of belief" as "generators of error" which ought to be "dismissed as sources of knowledge." Science, Pinker drones, is "hard," as in difficult to acquire, whereas tradition and faith are apparently squishy and easy to apprehend, understand, and affirm. What nonsense, Wieseltier responds, for reason "is larger than science," since reason contains science but goes beyond it. Tradition itself is a form of reason since it is "a body of accumulated innovations" emerging from acts of intelligence and reason looking for the best accounts of entire ranges of human concerns impenetrable to science without thereby becoming impenetrable to reason. Reason takes more than one path, because reality has more than one form.

## Many Roads of Reason

I've come to admire the thought of Luigi Giussani on the range of reason, about which he tartly remarks, "reason is not as arthritic or paralyzed as has been imagined by so much of modern philosophy. . . . Reason is much larger than this . . . it is agile, goes everywhere, travels many roads."[4] He does not mean this poetically, noting that the

[4] Luigi Giussani, *The Religious Sense*, trans. John Zucchi (Montreal & Kingston, ON: McGill-Queen's University Press, 1997), 17.

root of "method" in Greek, *met'hodon*, means "by the road." Reason travels many roads, that is, has many methods, because reality is rich. Method, he suggests, is determined by the nature of the object to be known rather than the knower's whim. Things are known according to their own mode, and some methods do not fit the nature of the knowable object. Consequently, since reality is rich, with depths and differentiations, so too reason develops polymorphically in response to various domains of the real.

We attempt to come to terms with reality "according to the totality of its factors," and we do so through reasonableness, "a mode of action that expresses and realizes reason, the capacity to become aware of reality." In this context, reasonableness does not mean moderation, as when we speak of a person being reasonable, or somewhat easy to get along with, disposed to give way on things that don't much matter, but rather human action by which we direct our reason through the performance of our intelligence to understand and know the real in its various forms. When we direct and perform reason in this way, we are always looking for reasons, for accounts and explanations—not just any kind of reason, but adequate reasons.

At this, a certain kind of thinker will leap into action, brandishing his epistemological cudgel to demand an account of the standards or criteria of adequate reasons, which misses the point entirely. The intellect seeks adequate reasons, of course, but this remains a heuristic, an anticipation or directedness of intellect towards its satisfaction or fulfillment, towards its act, where the content and standards of intellect are contextualized by the method used, and the method is determined by the object sought. No account of adequate reasons applies univocally to each method; each method develops its own account. Consider this very simple example: in elementary school I recall a frustrating teacher who demanded overly precise measurements of angles with a protractor. A protractor is a somewhat clumsy instrument in clumsy hands, and is more approximation than determination. Moved *ever so slightly* it can reasonably yield a measurement of either 48 or 49 degrees, but this teacher would mark an answer of 48 incorrect, insisting that the answer was 49 degrees. That's not reasonable, for the way we were attempting to find the answer simply doesn't demand, let alone allow, that kind of specificity. Naturally, when one is not measuring one angle but all three angles of a triangle even the protractor has some demands placed upon it. If the interior angles of the triangle were measured as 60, 61, and 63, something is amiss, and the difference matters significantly. In trigonometry even more precision is demanded, but it is the nature of the thing studied, and how it is studied, that determines what counts as an adequate reason. One does not ask for probability from a geometer or for certainty from a rhetorician, after all.

There is no meaningful universal account of "adequate reason" since it depends on what method is used, although I'm not suggesting that just any reason counts as adequate. Of course not. Some reasons are silly, others contradictory, some defeasible, others highly improbable, while yet others are likely, strong, or adequate. But the content and standards, the canon of rationality, are method-dependent. That an ecumenical council defined orthodoxy as $x$ and heresy as $y$ counts as an adequate reason to affirm $x$ and deny $y$ in the domain of dogma, but that a cardinal suggests $x$ rather than $y$ about science, politics, or economics... perhaps not. A Euclidean proof counts as an adequate reason in Euclidean geometry, but it does not follow that aesthetic judgments need axioms, deductions, and a necessary conclusion. The object determines the method, and the methods develop their own internal standards for what counts as an adequate reason

Giussani rejects any claims of one method to become the master all other methods must obey or mimic. Something could be reasonable in the sense of "demonstrable in the strict sense of the word," but it is "not true that the entire human experience of the reasonable is contained in this identification." One sees this mistake made whenever someone haughtily demands a proof for God's existence and means by this a demonstration equivalent in its certainty to showing your work in an algebra problem. The "most interesting, original aspects of reality" are not known by demonstration: it does not follow that they are irrational or unknowable or not known. Similarly, the reasonable is not conflated with logic. Logic has its place and functions on a certain model and heuristic of coherence and rigor, but it's slightly bizarre for a husband to request a logical syllogism of his wife so he can rest assured that she loves him. That is the wrong sense of reasonableness for the method, and for the objective known. (Perhaps logicians in love do such things, but in that case the syllogism is a sort of stilted love poem, but to each his own, I suppose.)

Reason is always enacted in a particular way, involving "many methods, procedures, or processes depending upon the type of object in question. Reason does not have a single method; it is polyvalent, rich, agile, and mobile," according to Giussani. Consequently, he identifies at least four basic methodologies, each with its own form of objectivity or account of adequate reasons: mathematics, science, philosophy, and a kind of moral certainty, and within these, subdivisions obviously occur, for there are multiple domains of science with each particular set of data, procedures, and canons. Reason is polyvalent because reality is polymorphic.

Of the four methods identified by Giussani, I suspect that of *moral certainty* is most opaque to us at first glance, but that we have at least some sense of the other three modes. This final method, he suggests, yields certainty about human behavior, although I would rather we keep to his earlier language of adequacy rather than certainty. Like the other methods, moral certainty is an exercise of intelligence; like the other methods, it grasps form and intelligibility in the instances, and some people are able to grasp intelligibility more readily and surely than others. We should not be surprised that some people have greater facility than do others, for this is the case in every method.

How do you know your spouse loves you? Wires testing heartrates and dopamine levels, a math formula, philosophical explorations of the definition and types of love? Those are dead ends, entirely unresponsive to the question whether *this* person loves *you*. We seek a moral and existential knowledge, and however unlike the knowledge of math, science, and philosophy, it's knowledge all the same, not subjectivism or wish. We pay attention to the phenomenon in experience, which gets a kind of shape or definition "in *understanding* something, discovering its meaning" and then making a judgment on the basis of some criterion. As much as we might wish that criterion to be so objective as to not involve ourselves, as if we could have moral knowledge without involving finite, fallible humans, Giussani correctly insists that the criterion is "inherent within us." That is, reason is part of our very nature as rational animals and pushes us, drives us, motivates us, to seek true judgment.

Since the criterion cannot be found outside of reason, as if free-floating in the universe, it is false to think objectivity in moral certainty is achieved when we are uninvolved or distant. Not at all. Instead, "I will be able to be certain about you, to the extent that I pay more attention to your life, that is, that I share in your life." Moral certainty about another's love requires paying attention to them, attending to them, in the sense of both moving close to them (I tend in your direction) and caring about them (tending to them, as one tends to a patient or a plant). Feeling and emotion are not hostile to objectivity, although feelings are not self-validating either; truth is not so objective as to preclude making a judgment. Truth, Aristotle reminds us, is not out there in the world somewhere as a property. Truth is a relationship between the world and the one who judges, and we can and often do judge incorrectly.

Consequently, we need pay attention not only to the one about whose love we wish to know, but also to ourselves, to our virtue and power of discernment. Giussani puts it this way: "the more powerfully one is human, the more one is able to become certain about another on the basis of only a few indications. . . . The more powerfully human one is, the more one is able to perceive with certainty. . . . The more one is truly human, the more one is able to trust, because one understands the reasons for believing in another." We should interpret this as requiring not the erasure of ourselves but instead the full flourishing and enactment of ourselves, for reason does not require the absence of all mediation in order to be true or certain.

If we imagine all knowing along the lines of the knowledge of bodies, mediation can certainly seem like a barrier, impediment, or distortion. If the knower, me, is *over here*, and the thing to be known is an already-out-there-now *over there*, knowing is like taking a look or seeing the thing clearly. When we attempt to see, mediation threatens to distort, because mediation implies the attempt to *look through* the mediation, and if the medium imparts something of itself into the vision we don't see the thing as it is, merely as it appears to us. Rose-colored glasses make everything seem pink, as it were.

But moral certainty is not a looking at an object over there; it is a kind of communion, for the "thing" known is not a thing at all, but a person. The knower and the known are both persons, both capable of giving themselves to be known and receiving the offer of friendship with the other. In this method, knowledge is much more like communion than staring, much more like friendship or the knowing of marriage than the close-up of a microscope. Our feelings reveal our values and mediate between us and the person we hope to know with moral certainty. We cannot help that, nor would we want it otherwise. If a man wonders if his wife loves him, and tries to ascertain this by means of bracketing or ignoring all of his tenderness and joy, he is trying to know his beloved without access to his own love. He is asking if his spouse loves him while using a method *as if* she is not his spouse but a stranger on the street, which would not make the knowledge in question more likely or certain but far less so. "The more something interests an individual" the more it generates feeling and the more "will reasoning, in the act of knowing that value in relation to our lives, be conditioned by this feeling."

We ought not conclude that feeling is valid just as such,

let alone replaces reasoning, but still knowing is conditioned by feeling, operates through and alongside feeling, and feeling needn't be considered a barrier between us and reality as much as a "hook" or "bridge" placing us into contact with reality, providing access. Recall, also, that the reality we are attempting here to know, the "object" we are considering in the fourth method of moral certainty, is not the world of science or math, but the world of value and persons. The world of value ought to prompt feeling. As Thomas notes, the good is well defined as "being insofar as it is desired," and the beautiful is "being insofar as it causes delight," to which we might add that the person is "being insofar as it freely offers communion." It is fitting, it is proper, that we have feelings as access points to the world of the good, the beautiful, and the personal. We will not have a dispassionate view of these realities, nor is it proper to do so.

If in the world of bodies objective knowing consists in something like a clear look, in the world of moral certainty it consists of love. Giussani describes the "morality of knowing" as follows: "*Love the truth . . . more than your attachment to the opinions you have already formed. . . .* More concisely one could say, 'love the truth more than yourself.'" Or, in the formulation of Alice von Hildebrand, a fundamental failure in human relationships is "the lack of *reverence* with which we tend to approach other persons."[5] In reverence, we learn to love people *as they are*—a realism—coming to know them with genuine receptivity. She suggests that in true love of the other, "true love pitilessly sees

<hr>

[5] Alice von Hildebrand, "Communion," in *The Art of Living* (Steubenville: Hildebrand Project, 2017), 43–59, at 47.

the faults and shortcomings of the loved one; but it will interpret these faults differently." She suggests that in love, knowing persons through Giussani's moral certainty, "all the good qualities of the beloved are considered to be a valid expression of his true self; whereas his faults"—which are pitilessly noted—"are interpreted as an unfaithfulness toward his true self." All the vices are seen as uncharacteristic of the person as they are in God's eyes, as they truly could be and become.

So described, the method of moral certainty prompts the question of faith, perhaps just *is* the question of faith, and Giussani links them closely. Faith is an adherence to what another affirms as true, he claims, and this might be reasonable or unreasonable. If in a judgment of moral certainty I conclude that the other has genuine knowledge, then my own commitment to that knowledge is coherent and consistent, although obviously I can be mistaken. There is some risk in this, although humans engage in such acts of faith frequently. Without such commitments humanity would be stuck, for development depends on the work of others, and it is impossible—not to mention ridiculous—to attempt to work out everything that humans have come to know. As such, the "question of moral certainty is the main problem of life," for on it depends not only many of my own commitments but also those of society and civilization. We can be mistaken in our moral certainties, just as we can be mistaken in our scientific, mathematical, and philosophical judgments, none of which calls into question the capacity or reasonability of affirming the genuine possibility that we can be correct in all these methods.

The tendency of our time, however, is reductionism about reason, towards viewing science as the only genuine basis for actual knowledge, and with science suggesting a deflationary sense of being. The human is really *nothing but* biology, biology is really nothing but chemistry, chemistry is nothing but physics, and physics is nothing but math. To understand the human without mystification is to understand the substrate, which is the actual cause, and anything resisting deflation is either not yet understood but awaits the proper reduction or is not understandable at all, merely convention or vitality or bias—flattened, imprisoned immanence.

In his Regensburg Address, Benedict XVI challenges this "modern self-limitation of reason," especially when "radicalized" by the natural sciences.[6] After explaining that God is *logos* and cannot act contrary to the *logos*, thus allowing for a generative synthesis between Christianity and the best of Greek thought, he suggests that the waves of dehellenization of doctrine have not restored Christianity to some pristine state of the early Church but rather abandoned reason to become a distorted version of itself. The modern vision of reason is an odd yoking of Cartesianism to empiricism, presupposing a mathematical form of matter open to rationality and allowing the efficient use of matter, as evidenced by the success of technology. Matter is useful and exploitable, but only falsification or verification by experiment "can yield decisive certainty." Consequently, *only* math and empirical evidence are scientific, and *only* science counts as the criterion of real knowing.

The question of God, quite obviously, doesn't fit this pattern and is jettisoned, not at the expense of God but of reason, which suffers "a reduction" of its scope and power. The

[6] Benedict XVI, "Faith, Reason, and the University: Memories and Reflections," University of Regensburg, Germany (September 12, 2006).

late pope does not suggest anything like turning back the clock or rejecting the accomplishments of the sciences, but instead a "broadening" of our understanding of reason, an expanded view not at all critical but restorative. In what I'm sure is a surprise to the cultured despisers of religion, Benedict argues first that reductive reason harms the dialogue of cultures since it attacks the "most profound convictions" of many people, including religious believers, and secondly that hiding from the insights and questions of religion harms reason by obscuring its ground. Consequently, it is people of "Biblical faith," not the practitioners of so-called neutral or procedural rationality, who are the defenders of reason in its full measure, and a central responsibility of people of faith is helping reason to attain its own measure. In our moment, Athens has become a ghostly version of itself, unable to recover with its own resources. Jerusalem and Rome help Athens fulfill its full range by asking all the relevant questions in all the relevant ways. This is not to convert or change Athens into Jerusalem or Rome, but to help Athens be itself. Reason is locked into a very small room, unable to escape, and needs faith to be reason again. This is no surprise. Grace presupposes nature, but grace also heals and perfects nature *qua* nature long before elevating it to its supernatural fulfillment.

⊕

In this and the previous chapter, I suggest non-idyllic alternatives to the malaises of immanence. The Thomistic tradition is more than capable of providing a dynamic ontology and a lively cognitional theory able to avoid the flattering tendencies of modernity and the concomitant trajectory of despair. Still, while good ontology and cognitional theory might avoid despair, they aren't cause for hope. Hope is a theological virtue, a grace, not a human accomplishment. Grace builds upon and perfects nature, to be sure, so good philosophy smooths the way for hope without providing hope itself. To hope I turn in the final chapter.

# 9

## Hope

BERNARD LONERGAN suggests, much as Giussani does, that faith is knowledge brought forth of religious love.[1] If moral certainty, and natural faith/trust as an instance of it, is happily entangled with love of truth and love of the person, then faith in its particular theological meaning is caught up into the discussion. As Lonergan suggests, faith is a sort of knowledge which has as its cause "God's love flooding our hearts" (Rom 5:5). In this, not only do we find something similar to what we apprehend in our tending for society, culture, and persons, but "there is added an apprehension of transcendent value." In God's love flooding our hearts through the Holy Spirit, we apprehend something outside the locked room, outside the awful monad of immanence Ferrante depicts. Such apprehension is not merely another value among values but corresponds to our dynamic desire for all goodness, truth, and being, it is an "actuated orientation towards the mystery of love and awe." What we have by nature reached for but have been entirely unable by nature to grasp is now actuated, albeit dependent on the agency of God and His love given to us.

---

[1] Bernard Lonergan, *Method in Theology* (New York: Seabury Press, 1972), 115–19.

The human is the strangest of all creatures. Like all other creatures, we seek our act and our fullness, which includes seeking to communicate that act as far as possible, but as persons we alone are created for our own sake, and thus are disproportionate to the rest of the natural world. Oddly, perplexingly, we are natural beings and not in any way God-stuff or divine, and, yet, while all things seek in their way to return to God, we as persons, and thus created in the image of God, seek to return to God in keeping with that image. Consequently, alone of all creation we have a nature which reaches out towards a supernatural vocation that cannot be fulfilled by any agent within nature. We are restless until resting in God, and we have a natural desire for something beyond nature, and thus seek to outstrip ourselves, which we cannot of ourselves do. To be a person is always to be ontologically rich and poor. Rich because like all being we have a nature to fulfill and to communicate; poor because we, like everything except God, are not in full actuality; radically rich and radically poor in that our nature is capacious enough to seek unity with God in a personal way, but cannot accomplish that in any way by its own power.

In Lonergan's language, the human is a self-transcending being. As persons, we have an interiority unique among animals, for we are personal subjects capable of self-directedness. Interiority is not self-enclosed, not at all like an atom or a monad without windows and doors to the good, true, and beautiful, but has an exigence, a drive, to know, choose, and love that which is other than itself. Knowing is a kind of self-transcendence where we wish to grasp things as they are, in the mode of the object rather than our opinion of the object. Authentic choosing is the attempt to actualize the world of genuine value rather than our own satisfactions, and thus transcends mere pleasure and comfort. In love we seek to will the good of the other and to enter into union with them, whether in friendship, marriage, the sacraments, or the kingdom of God. We are the being longing for membership, longing to participate with the world, with other persons, and with the Divine Persons.

This should not surprise us. We are in the image of God the Holy Trinity—one Being in three persons. Those persons are intrinsically relational. All three are equally and consubstantially God and yet have distinct relations to each other. The Father is God, the Son is God, the Holy Spirit is God, but the Father is neither the Son nor the Spirit, the Son is neither the Father nor the Spirit, and the Spirit is neither the Father nor the Son. One being in distinct relations distinguishing the persons. The Father is the begetter, the Son the begotten, and the Spirit spirates from the Father and the Son. The Father as begetter communicates the entirety of the Godhead to the Son, holding nothing back, keeping nothing in reserve, yet losing nothing. He pours forth the entirety of his being and remains God. The Son receives the entirety of this communication, the infinite act and divine being of the Father, and his reception is perfect, losing none of the Godhead and not in any way less than God because receiving. The relationship of endless giving, receiving, and giving-back of love between the Father and Son is so perfect as to spirate a third relation, the Spirit, who is equal to the others in being. Three persons in relation; it is entirely fitting to consider the term *person* not as we do an *individual*—a unity-identity-whole unto itself—but rather as substance in relation, as a category intrinsically and essentially relational in meaning. Persons are not closed off and walled into their subjectivity.

Persons are by definition self-transcending beings, reaching out to others and to all things in light of personhood.

Human persons exist in relationship even to themselves. That is, "person" means something distinct from essence. Humans may be well defined as rational animals, but if we assume that on the traditional definition of "person" as used by Boethius and Aquinas—individual substance of a rational nature—we are dealing only with an *essence*, a quiddity, a *whatness*, then we have misunderstood the term. It is substance in relation, not static substance closed in and completed in itself. A person is not only a *what* but a *who*: prior to relating to others, he relates to himself. Persons are self-governed, after all, and while this means nothing like Kantian autonomy or Sartrean self-creation, since we do have a nature given to us by God and essentially true and constitutive of our being, we can also relate to our own essence in different ways, because free. This is why we can choose to be inhuman, to act like a beast. We cannot be non-human or transform ourselves into mere animals, for we are by definition rational animals and cannot be otherwise, but in choice we can act unintelligently, irrationally, unreasonably, and so choose to act *as if* something other than we are, to act *contra* our nature. To be inhuman, bestial.[2]

The human always has before him the grand drama of choosing life or death. Persons have this choice in how they relate to themselves—will they accept their own nature given to them by God, as rational and thus capable of choosing against their nature? Humans have this choice

[2] These are ideas I learned from Robert Spaemann, *Persons: The Difference between "Someone" and "Something,"* trans. Oliver O'Donovan (Oxford: Oxford University Press, 2006).

160

also in their capacities of knowing and acting—will they seek opinion and satisfaction or, in self-transcendence, the true and the good? Persons have this choice with respect to others—will they love neighbor, will they love God?

So it is that when the love of God floods our heart through the gift of the Holy Spirit we are given the possibility of self-transcendence, now a self-transcendence prompted and enabled by a personal agent fundamentally transcendent of the universe. This divine agent calls forth the possibility of the supernatural vocation proper to us but outstripping our ability to actualize it, and yet never actualized without our cooperation. God's love given prompts an ineluctable question demanding my decision: "Will I love Him in return, or will I refuse? Will I live out the gift of His love, or will I hold back, turn away, withdraw?"[3] Such withdrawal is a profound rejection, though, since to reject this love, to reject faith, is to shrink back from the embrace and knowledge of transcendent value, the transcendent goodness of God.

As Lonergan describes it, the gift of faith, religious knowledge born from God's love flooding us, apprehends transcendent, absolute value, placing "all other values in the light and the shadow of transcendent" goodness. Seen in the light of transcendent value, all temporal and earthly values are magnified and glorified, seen as truly and really good because participating in and sustained by the divine goodness. Simultaneously, however, they are placed in a kind of shadow, recognized as non-ultimate and derivative. Of real value, in other words, but not ultimate.

---

[3] Lonergan, *Method*, 116.

Without the light of faith, the exclusive humanism described in earlier chapters is all there is, and the immanent frame is a closed one, or, in Lonergan's terms, "the originating value is man and the terminal value is the human good man brings about." That is, without faith all that remains is exclusive humanism, the tyranny of mastery, rationalistic plans, activism, inner-worldly religions, and all the pathologies explored in the earlier chapters of this book. The human becomes the source and end of action, the only place of value and intention in the entire universe, and yet as merely another part of a universe devoid of value our own intentions are also devoid of substantial purpose. Faith, conversely, places our human concerns in a sort of shadow, revealing them as non-ultimate and contingent, and yet not *merely* human but caught up into a divine light and love also concerned with human things—so concerned as to become man and join in those same ordinary, human concerns and elevate and glorify them through the work and person of Jesus Christ. Since even the human works of Jesus, those of his human nature, have the Divine Person of the Son as their source, his human acts are caught up into the mission of the Second Person of the Trinity and sanctified beyond earthly measure. The human good participates in ultimate meaning and purpose.

Lonergan observes that "human development" can remain human without sinking into exclusive humanism since our full development, our full vocation, includes "holiness." God's love draws out a new "efficacy in all goodness, and the limit of human expectation ceases to be the grave." Faith places "human efforts in a friendly universe; it recalls an ultimate significance in human achievement," recognizing that "man's good also is God's glory." Without

faith, we have exclusive humanism and its frenzy and terror, like Olga trapped in a room without hope, as death
awaits; others are burdens; there is no way out, and no
father to assist us.

## Substantial Hope

Some of us, however, have hope. In the remarkable encycli-
cal *Spe salvi*, Benedict XVI explores the meaning of the
phrase *spe salvi facti sumus*, "in hope we were saved" (Rom
8:24). Redemption is not done or completed as a fact we
comfortably settle into; instead, it "is offered to us in the
sense that we have been given hope, trustworthy hope. . . ."
St Paul's formulation can pull us up short; the historical
dispute generally concerns the relationship of faith to salvation, but Benedict suggests that for Paul faith and hope are
virtually interchangeable, with the "fullness of faith" linked
to "the confession of our hope" (Heb 10:22–23). Faith
reveals that life will not end in the grave or in pointlessness,
and so the future, the *eschaton*, is known as good rather
than fearsome or empty. It is possible "to live the present as
well," however difficult that happens to be.

Christianity conveys more than content, more than a
series of revealed ideas not known before, for "the Christian
message was not only 'informative' but 'performative.'"
Certainly the Christian message has ideas—Benedict is not
ignoring the deposit of faith—but the Gospel communication "is one that makes things happen and is life-changing,"
especially by casting light into the darkness of the future
and thereby granting new life not only for the hereafter but
for now. Whatever happens, "I am awaited by this Love."

Ordinary human actions are given meaning by an expectation of love now and in the future. Christianity is not a

promise of social revolution and immanent perfection. Those aspirations place more on this world and our action than they can possibly bear, as evidenced by the hopeless frenzy of our own time, including the frenzy of those in the Church who should know better but have reduced the Gospel to social activism. Christian hope is performative in that it brings "an encounter with the Lord of all lords, an encounter with the living God and thus an encounter with a hope stronger" than any suffering, "a hope which therefore transformed life and the world from within." It is not the laws of nature, those things properly sought and understood by science, which govern the world, not ultimately, nor is it the impersonal unmoved mover of providential deism, but the final say is had by "reason, will, love—a Person," and thus we are not "slaves of the universe and of its law, we are free."

As Benedict teaches, a misunderstanding of hope by some Christians has deformed the truth. In Hebrews we are told that "faith is the *hypostasis* of things hoped for; the proof of things not seen" (11:1). He leaves *hypostasis* untranslated, since much depends on its interpretation. The medievals translated *hypostasis* as *substantia*, substance, and stressed the "proof" or *argumentum* aspect of hope. Faith is the *substance* of things hoped for, the *proof* of things not seen. On this reading, faith, which is an infused virtue, a stable disposition of the person resulting from grace, "takes root in us and reason is led to consent to what it does not see." That is, faith gives to us *now and already*, really gives and makes present, the things that are hoped for, namely salvation and true life. But this true life is already present, and we have a proof or a certainty of those things we hope for because that life is infused in us, we are already now possessing the merits of Christ through adoption. The life of Christ is given to us already, so that the Father might love in us what He loved in the Son.[4] Since this life is present substantially, it is known; its reality is its evidence, or proof.

Martin Luther, and eventually even many Catholic translators, fundamentally changed and weakened the text, Benedict notes. Luther being strongly opposed to the doctrine of infusion, his account of adoption was so enervated as to virtually transform it into a legal fiction of innocence without real filiation. Consequently, *hypostasis* for Luther has no sense of objective substance or present reality but rather "the subjective sense, as an expression of an interior attitude, and so, naturally, he also had to understand the term *argumentum* as a disposition of the subject." Hope transforms from an objective encounter with the life of Christ present in us into a subjective *hopefulness*, a mood, a commitment—into optimism. Or into faith as "standing firm in what one hopes, being convinced of what one does not see." These two translations of Hebrews 10 are not remotely similar in meaning, for one is about the objective work of Christ and the other about our subjective commitments. Luther's reading cannot but entail "merely a personal reaching out toward things to come that are still totally absent." Cue despair or activism.

Instead of optimism, activism, and the despair which follows, Benedict insists that faith "draws the future into the present," really and actually present not as an attitude but as property given from the Father to His *really and completely* adopted children, those who were not only legally His but

---

[4] See Preface VII of the Sundays in Ordinary Time: *". . . ut amares in nobis quod diligebas in Filio. . . ."*

had become incorporated into His life, so that they—we—
could live in this world with a persevering patience. Without such patience, we cannot but frantically reach for an
unknown and unreal "eternal life," "and yet we know that
all we can experience or accomplish is not what we yearn
for. This unknown 'thing' is the true 'hope' which drives us,
and at the same time the fact that it is unknown is the cause
of all forms of despair and also of all efforts . . . directed
toward worldly authenticity and human authenticity."

I won't rehearse it here, as it would repeat earlier sections
of this book, but Benedict provides a remarkably succinct
and powerful history of the distortion of Christian hope
into an ideological vision in which science and technique
are thought sufficient to undo original sin and provide
redemption, all while bettering our lot on earth. From early
modern science to Marx to the soul-wearying vision of
exclusive humanism, no such effort provides hope, for none
gives the substance of God's own life in divine filiation. The
hope of persons cannot be established through external
goods and structures, since life "is a relationship," as we
would expect given our personal nature, with "Him who is
the source of life." Further, to be brought into the life of
Christ is to be in communion with all others, to be drawn
"into his *being for others*." Absent this, our sense of being for
others transforms into the idea of progress, and since "there
is no God to create justice, it seems man himself is now
called on to establish it," with the impossible demand that
"man can and must do what no God actually does or is able
to do." But a world which attempts to create its own ultimate justice is a world without hope, he states, since a
world without the final redemption and vindication of the
Last Judgment is one in which our actions futilely attempt

to bear a weight entirely beyond their capacity. Against this, as Lonergan notes, the world in which transcendent meaning is encountered in love, in faith, and in hope is a friendly universe, one in which there is an ultimate significance to even our feeble and faltering efforts because those efforts are caught up into and sanctified by the divine work. But those works of ours need not be frantic, because they participate in an eternal life which is already ours rather than attempting to construct hope from nothing or create meaning out of meaninglessness.

In earlier chapters, I've suggested that the loss of transcendence has given us over to counsels of despair and that various ersatz forms of "hope" cannot deliver but are themselves instances and forms of despair. Humans are often in despair even when they don't know or believe themselves to be despairing; the human despairs whenever "severing his metaphysical link with existence, his umbilical link with being."[5] Only persons can despair, for only persons can relate falsely to their nature and its divine source, and humans thus often despair, sometimes consciously and sometimes otherwise.

The world is generous and friendly, made for persons and their relationality. The world is perhaps not enchanted, but it is an unfolding universe of substance for relation because the Triune Communion has ordered it towards communion with the human person. The world is not made for atoms or monads, nor does the law of the universe allow such monads to coexist somehow, held in check in their isolated sovereignty so as to not harm each other.

---

[5] Alice von Hildebrand, "Hope," in *The Art of Living* (Steubenville: Hildebrand Project, 2017), 61–77.

All the false forms of hope become forms of imprison-
ment and despair. They cement our isolation and forlorn-
ness, like Olga's reinforced door, constructed to keep out
her husband but now the source of her confinement. All
our tools, so beneficial when kept in their proper place, can
promise hope without the love of God, a freedom like that
of a "man who prefers his own despair to being helped out
of it" and, far "from being free in the deepest sense of the
term, is actually imprisoned in the cramp of an ego that has
become the caricature of an *imago Dei*; shrunken in itself,
turning ceaselessly upon itself" like a "man in prison."
Hope cannot function, cannot exist, without transcendence, without love allowing our self-transcendence.

All our false hopes attempt to ground themselves in *hope
that* something will happen, *that* a cure will appear, *that* the
policy will deliver, or *that* the plan comes to fruition. This is
the hopefulness of scientism, rationalism, inner-worldli-
ness, fundamentalism, and false enchantments. Hope cannot long survive such optimism, as evidenced by the
hopelessness of our own epoch despite its many material
advantages and comforts. Optimism, as described by Marcel, is merely "camouflaged sentimentality" that quickly
turns into a counsel of despair, suggesting that "wisdom is
early to despair," in the words of Gerard Manley Hopkins,
since in the end "nothing can be done / To keep at bay / Age
and age's evils, hoar hair, / Ruck and wrinkle, drooping,
dying, death's worst winding… / So be beginning, be beginning, to despair."[6] Marcel drives the point home: "As for
death, from this objective and functional point of view it

[6] Gerard Manley Hopkins, "The Leaden Echo and the Golden Echo"
(1879).

appears only as ceasing to function, falling into total useless-
ness, becoming sheer *waste* to be discarded. There is no need
to stress the atmosphere of suffocating sadness secreted by a
world whose main axis is functions."[7]

Instead, as Hildebrand and Marcel both insist, genuine
*hope that* requires a foundation of *hope in*, of hope in a person. Only hope in God allows me to see "with pitiless clarity that, humanly speaking, a situation is desperate; . . . but
I rely on an extra-mundane factor, and thus *refuse to see tragedy as the last word.* I break through the circle of immanent
causalities, and transcend to a sphere in which the pitiless
unfolding of immanent laws ceases to hold sway." When I
hope in God, I not only transcend myself and my own limited power, which often can do very little, even if rushing
about in wild activity in avoidance of this fact, but now I
hope in one beyond immanence and its severe limits and
scarcities. In faith His love pours new life even now, granting a share of His own eternal life, and the circle of immanence is broken. Marcel puts it as follows: "Hope consists
in asserting that there is at the heart of being, beyond all
data, beyond all inventories and all calculations, a mysteri-
ous principle in connivance with me, which cannot but will
what I will, at least if what I will is really worth willing and
is, in fact, willed with my whole being. . . . [R]eality *is* with
me in willing that it be so. I am not just wishing, I am
asserting; and this is what I . . . call the prophetic resonance
of genuine hope." To make the same point, Hopkins offers

[7] Gabriel Marcel, "Concrete Approaches to Investigating the Ontological Mystery," in *Gabriel Marcel's Perspectives on The Broken World*,
trans. Katharine Rose Hanley (Milwaukee: Marquette University Press,
1998), 174.

a rejoinder to the counsels of despair in the early sections of his poem, noting instead that "there is one, yes I have one...;/Only not within seeing of the sun,/... Somewhere elsewhere there is ah well where! One/... Yonder, yes yonder, yonder,/Yonder."

All that is immanent is contingent and destined for death, all is halfway between being and non-being. On this no real hope can rest, and all hopes-*that* flicker and fail. But in faith's substance of things hoped for, in the hope springing from the love of God poured into our hearts, we can refuse to be enclosed; by virtue of hoping *in* God all our hopes-*that* have being and fecundity. We hope in a God who created, sustained, and redeemed the world, and who is the origin and end of all, and who does not will that any should perish, who hates nothing He has created, and who came among us that there would be life abundant. We hope in a Father who pours out His goodness, who seeks to communicate His goodness as much as possible, and with Him all is possible. We hope in a God who sows even in the rocky soil, for His generosity knows no bounds, and He is infinite in wealth.

Hope is not resignation, but the condition and ground of all our actions. A friendly universe is a generative universe and requires the utmost of our attention, intelligence, reason, and responsibility. Hope does not do an end-run around our responsibility and our cooperation but allows them to be fruitful, albeit without the hint of the illusion of mastery or its tyranny, without the pretenses of rationalism, the frenzied pointlessness of denuded nature, or the idylls of faux-enchantments. Instead, hope allows us to grow into the full stature of the children of God, capable of act, of becoming an acting person. As Thomas Aquinas knew,

God's providence determines not only what will happen but *how* it will happen, and God has determined that much will happen through our own freedom. *All* our self-constitution as agents requires our act, nor can it be otherwise. So we are set free to act, in hope, without illusion, anxiety, fear, frenzy, or despair.

We act as the sons and daughters of God, knowing that all that is His is ours. We are free to play those serious games that happy children play, knowing that they must play as well as they can, as hard as they can, for as long as they can, but in the end a Father will lead them home, unlock the door (which was never stuck to begin with), and keep us under His care—far fonder than we would have ever had for ourselves.

# Conclusion

## *Spes Nostra*

MY ACCOUNT BEGAN with the story of two mothers in the fiction of Elena Ferrante: Leda, with a revulsion and horror at pregnancy and a desire to expel the filth of a child, and Olga, trapped in the radical immanence of her own enclosed life, the prison of herself and her children. Olga is terrified of turning into the *poverella*, the woman who is poor, who doesn't matter, who disappears from sight. For these women, life is hopeless. Not only are they confined within the immanence of a world without God, but the normal things of life such as marriage and children are for them sources of despair and disgust rather than joy, love, hope—they lack even simple natural optimism on the socio-biological level.

Ferrante's novels are bleak; my friends and I disagree on their value. One friend thinks they are without redemptive worth, just pain and pointlessness. Another, like me, thinks they depict, with honest realism, a world in which religion is absent and the inner-worldly religions of Marxism, science, political action, humanities, art, and a certain kind of feminism are revealed as impotent and vain. Vanity of vanities. There are no idylls in Ferrante. I know nothing of the actual author of these novels—recall that it's a pen name and no one is sure who it is—but I savor the idea that she is a Catholic who recognizes that there is very little reason to

172

accommodate and bend ourselves to the whims of the modern world, now that that world loathes and detests itself almost completely. The false visions of progress, science, political ideologies, utopias, and exclusive humanism are exposed and unmasked. Ours is a hopeless age and thus an age of great opportunity for the Gospel. From a human point of view things seem bleak for the Church and the Faith; from a supernatural point of view ours is a time of remarkable clarity. Idols are known to be idols, so perhaps we might try proclaiming the one true God.

Recently, an undergraduate remarked to me that many of her peers hope to disappear and render themselves invisible, despite the endless selfies and posting of same on social media. Her description brought to mind the opening passages of the novel for which Ferrante is most famous, *My Brilliant Friend,* in which the brilliant friend does not fear disappearance and invisibility but seeks it, longs for it, as a kind of vindication. Olga fears becoming the *poverella,* but Lila hopes for it. She hopes, as the prologue to the novel is called, to find salvation by "eliminating all the traces."[1] Of Lila, her friend Lenù says:

> It's been at least three decades since she told me that she wanted to disappear without leaving a trace, and I'm the only one who knows what she means. She never had in mind any sort of flight, a change of identity, the dream of making a new life somewhere else. And she never thought of suicide, repulsed by the idea that Rino [her son] would have anything to do with her body. . . . She meant something different: she

[1] Elena Ferrante, *My Brilliant Friend,* trans. Ann Goldstein (New York: Europa Editions, 2012).

wanted to vanish; she wanted every one of her cells to disappear, nothing of her ever to be found. And since I know her well, or at least I think I know her, I take it for granted that she has found a way to disappear, to leave not so much as a hair anywhere in this world.

Not hope for another world, not hope of another life, not even the odd hope that suicide would bring a kind of relief in the end of pain—just an elimination of all traces of her existence.

According to Aquinas, insofar as a being is good it seeks to communicate itself. In light of such a metaphysics, the desire to eliminate all traces, to communicate nothing, not even to communicate one's absence but to remove all hint of communication, suggests the privation of goodness. Perhaps it is no accident the epigraph to *My Brilliant Friend* cites Goethe's remark that the author creates "as Devil."

If many of the young seek to render themselves invisible, to eliminate their traces, they must be extremely sad, without hope in this world. In a sense, they might know better than some of their parents and grandparents still believing in the idols of politics, -isms, progress, and all the other promises which the young find so empty. Better to vanish than believe in what is obviously utter rot—unmasked idylls don't provide much comfort. On the other hand, I encounter many other college students attempting their best to hope *that* politics will deliver, that the perfect administrative state, a vision of the common good, or some eastern European country can provide succor for their weary souls. They will soon be disappointed, I expect, for no idylls last long.

Hope is found *in* the yonder; in the One who transcends us and is so transcendent as to be closer to us than we are to

ourselves without interfering or competing with our freedom, for He is not just another entity among entities. So
transcendent as to become one of us and yet not lose his
divine personhood, and thereby allow all human self-transcendence towards what is genuine hope. He has gone
before us, he has done what we have done. He was born,
grew, learned, worked, studied, had friends, loved his
friends, wept, drank wine, rejoiced, and died. He has done
what we do, and his life can be ours; our new life is the substance of things hoped for. His life is eternal life, and his
life is our own, and so we hope. We will not vanish, but
will become more real, more visible, more known, more
communicated as his life saturates our own. We become
hidden in him, but when he appears we will appear with
him in glory (Col 3:1–4). When he appears, we appear, and
it is in his glory that we become fully alive, alive with eternal life. Thus we hope. In hope we act, but not in activism
or despair. We become ourselves, for the first time, really,
and we act in freedom.

There is no better image of such freedom than a mother.
Not any mother, but our Mother, Our Lady. To the possibility of motherhood she says, Let it be, and rejoices.
Notice how she acts. This is not passivity. She ponders, she
questions, and she accepts. Unlike Zachariah who when
told that his barren wife Elizabeth would give birth to John
the Baptist was troubled and afraid and demanded proof,
and was struck silent by the angel in consequence, the Virgin, full of grace, affirms the message, says yes—*fiat*—and
asks only *how* it will be accomplished, since she is a virgin,
without denying *that* it is true. Zachariah doubts that it is
true, she accepts that it is true and wonders how it will be.
And her soul magnifies the Lord and knows that all genera-

tions shall call her blessed (Luke 1:1–5). She has hope and is a source of hope. *Sancta Maria, spes nostra*: holy Mary, our hope. She does not disappear. All generations remember and call her blessed. She does not reject her child with loathing, and thus we all have hope.

In Genesis 2, it's notable that only Adam speaks when he first encounters Eve, leading some critics to protest her passivity and silence. Adam rejoices: "At last! Bone of my bone and flesh of my flesh," but Eve says not a word. But those critics fail to understand the full story. The second Eve speaks definitively, and her speaking, her *fiat*, are the most important words ever spoken, for they are the very possibility of any hope for us. She chooses, and becomes our hope. We have our own choice to make. In the words of Henry Adams, the options are either "the dynamo" of modern scientism or "the virgin." Either Francis Bacon and all his frustrated epigones, or Our Lady. A vanishing barrenness or life. Immanence or self-transcendence.

Despair or hope.

# Bibliography

"Commitment (The Woo Woo Issue)." *Los Angeles Times* (August 2022). https://www.latimes.com/projects/commitment/.

Aristotle. *Nicomachean Ethics*. Translated by Terence Irwin. Indianapolis: Hackett Publishing, 1999.

Benedict XVI. "Faith, Reason, and the University: Memories and Reflections." Regensburg, Germany, September 12, 2006. https://www.vatican.va/content/benedict-xvi/en/speeches/2006/september/documents/hf_ben-xvi_spe_20060 912_university-regensburg.html.

Burton, Tara Isabella. "Bad Traditionalism." *Commonweal* (July 6, 2020). https://www.commonwealmagazine.org/bad-traditionalism.

———. "Christianity Gets Weird." *New York Times* (May 8, 2020). https://www.nytimes.com/2020/05/08/opinion/sunday/weird-christians.html.

*Catechism of the Catholic Church*, 2nd edition. Washington, DC: United States Catholic Conference, 1987.

Clarke, W. Norris. "Person, Being, and St Thomas." *Communio* 19 (1992): 601–18.

Del Noce, Augusto. *The Crisis of Modernity*. Translated by Carlo Lancellotti. Montreal & Kingston, ON: McGill-Queen's University Press, 2014.

Derrida, Jacques. *Rogues: Two Essays on Reason*. Translated by Pascale-Anne Brault and Michael Naas. Stanford, CA: Stanford University Press, 2005.

Eagleton, Terry. *Culture and the Death of God*. New Haven, CT: Yale University Press, 2014.

Ferrante, Elena. *The Lost Daughter.* Translated by Ann Goldstein. New York: Europa, 2008.

———. *The Days of Abandonment.* Translated by Ann Goldstein. New York: Europa, 2005.

———. *My Brilliant Friend.* Translated by Ann Goldstein. New York: Europa, 2012.

Ferry, Luc. *A Brief History of Thought: A Philosophical Guide to Living.* Translated by Theo Cuffe. New York: Harper Perennial, 2011.

Gilson, Etienne. *The Spirit of Medieval Philosophy.* Translated by A. H. C. Downes. South Bend, IN: University of Notre Dame Press, 1991.

Giussani, Luigi. *The Religious Sense.* Translated by John Zucchi. Montreal & Kingston, ON: McGill-Queen's University Press, 1997.

Gricoski, Thomas. *Being Unfolded: Edith Stein on the Meaning of Being.* Washington, DC: Catholic University of America Press, 2020.

Hanson, Molly. "Could Neo-paganism be the New 'Religion' of America?" *Big Think* (September 30, 2019). https://bigthink.com/the-present/modern-paganism/.

Harari, Yuval Noah. *Homo Deus: A Brief History of Tomorrow.* New York: Harper, 2017.

Harari, Yuval Noah and Daniel Kahneman. "Death Is Optional: A Conversation." *Edge* (March 4, 2015). https://www.edge.org/conversation/yuval_noah_harari-daniel_kahneman-death-is-optional.

Hildebrand, Alice von. *The Art of Living.* Steubenville: Hildebrand Project, 2017.

Hitchens, Peter. "Alice's Oxford." *First Things* (November 10, 2017). https://www.firstthings.com/web-exclusives/2017/11/alices-oxford.

Hopkins, Gerard Manley. "As Kingfishers Catch Fire." 1877.

————. "The Leaden Echo and the Golden Echo." 1879.

Jacobs, Alan. "Fantasy and the Buffered Self." *The New Atlantis* (Winter 2014). https://www.thenewatlantis.com/publications/fantasy-and-the-buffered-self.

Jonas, Hans. *Philosophical Essays: From Ancient Creed to Technological Man.* Englewood Cliffs, NJ: Prentice-Hall, 1974.

Jones, David. *The Anathemata: Fragments of an Attempted Writing.* London: Faber and Faber, 1952.

Legutko, Ryszard. *The Demon in Democracy: Totalitarian Temptations in Free Societies.* Translated by Teresa Adelson. New York: Encounter Books, 2016.

Lewis, C. S. *That Hideous Strength.* New York: Scribner, 2003.

Lonergan, Bernard. *Method in Theology.* New York: Seabury Press, 1972.

————. *Insight: A Study of Human Understanding.* London: Darton, Longman, and Todd, 1973.

————. *A Second Collection.* Toronto: University of Toronto Press, 1974.

Manent, Pierre. *Metamorphoses of the City: On the Western Dynamic.* Translated by Marc LePain. Cambridge, MA: Harvard University Press, 2013.

————. *Natural Law and Human Rights: Toward a Recovery of Practical Reason.* Translated by Ralph C. Hancock. South Bend, IN: University of Notre Dame Press, 2020.

————. *The Religion of Humanity: The Illusion of Our Times.* Translated by Paul Seaton. South Bend, IN: St. Augustine's Press, 2022.

Marcel, Gabriel. "Concrete Approaches to Investigating the Ontological Mystery." In *Gabriel Marcel's Perspectives on The Broken World.* Translated by Katharine Rose Hanley.

Milwaukee: Marquette University Press, 1998.

Mason, Charlotte. "Three Educational Idylls." *The Parents' Review* 23 (1912): 801–11.

McClay, Wilfred. "The Illusion of Mastery: Man and Authority." *The City* (Spring 2011): 20–30.

Newman, John Henry. *An Essay on the Development of Christian Doctrine.* South Bend, IN: University of Notre Dame Press, 1994.

Oakeshott, Michael. *Rationalism in Politics and Other Essays.* Indianapolis: Liberty Fund, 1991.

Peters, Mark. "The Norse Gods' Unlikely Comeback." *Boston Globe* (November 4, 2017). https://www.bostonglobe.com/ideas/2017/11/04/the-norse-gods-unlikely-comeback/8w8mYFuWedi4qPEzjxBBsI/story.html.

Percy, Walker. *Lost in the Cosmos: The Last Self-Help Book.* New York: Picador, 1983.

Plato. *The Republic of Plato.* Translated by Allan Bloom. New York: Basic Books, 1968.

Quinones, Julian and Arijeta Lajka. "What kind of society do you want to live in? Inside the country where Down syndrome is disappearing." *CBS News* (August 15, 2017). https://www.cbsnews.com/news/down-syndrome-iceland/.

Rieff, Philip. *My Life among the Deathworks: Illustrations of the Aesthetics of Authority.* Charlottesville: University of Virginia Press, 2006.

Rorty, Richard. *Philosophy and Social Hope.* New York: Penguin Books, 1999.

Scola, Angelo. *Let's Not Forget God: Freedom of Faith, Culture, and Politics.* New York: Image, 2014.

Scruton, Roger. *Conservatism: An Invitation to the Great Tradition.* New York: All Points Books, 2017.

Second Vatican Council. *Dignitatis humanae*, Declaration on Religious Freedom. December 7, 1965. https://www.vatican.va/archive/hist_councils/ii_vatican_council/documents/vat-ii_decl_19651207_dignitatis-humanae_en.html.

Smith, Steven D. *The Disenchantment of Secular Discourse.* Cambridge, MA: Harvard University Press, 2010.

Snell, R.J. *Acedia and Its Discontents: Metaphysical Boredom in an Empire of Desire.* (Kettering, OH: Angelico Press, 2015).

———. "Don't Panic." *Public Discourse* (August 30, 2022). https://www.thepublicdiscourse.com/2022/08/84171/.

———. "Hang On! Faith and Sexual Ethics." *Public Discourse* (October 11, 2022). https://www.thepublicdiscourse.com/2022/10/85020/.

———. "How Should Conservatives Respond to Revolution?" *Public Discourse* (April 4, 2023). https://www.thepublicdiscourse.com/2023/04/88212/.

———. "Lost in the Chaos: The Danger of Total Politics." *Public Discourse* (August 19, 2021). https://www.thepublicdiscourse.com/2021/08/77247/.

———"The Truth of Sensible Politics." *Public Discourse* (May 15, 2023). https://www.thepublicdiscourse.com/2023/05/88831/.

Snell, R.J. and Robert P. George. *Mind, Heart, and Soul: Intellectuals and the Path to Rome.* Charlotte, NC: TAN Books, 2018.

Spaemann, Robert. *Persons: The Difference between "Someone" and "Something."* Translated by Oliver O'Donovan. Oxford: Oxford University Press, 2006.

Taylor, Charles. *A Secular Age.* Cambridge, MA: Belknap Press, 2007.

Thomas Aquinas. *De ente et essentia.* Translated by Robert T.

Miller. *Medieval Sourcebook*: Fordham University, 1997. https://sourcebooks.fordham.edu/basis/aquinas-esse.asp.

Voegelin, Eric. *Modernity without Restraint. The Collected Works of Eric Voegelin*, Volume 5. Edited by Manfred Henningsen. Columbia, MO: University of Missouri Press, 2000.

———. "Reason: The Classic Experience." In *Anamnesis*. Translated by Gerhart Niemeyer. Columbia, MO: University of Missouri Press, 1978: 89–115.

Wieseltier, Leon. "Crimes against Humanities." *The New Republic* (September 3, 2013). https://newrepublic.com/article/114548/leon-wieseltier-responds-steven-pinkers-scientism.

Wood, Graeme. "How Bronze Age Pervert Charmed the Far Right." *The Atlantic* (September 2023). https://www.theatlantic.com/magazine/archive/2023/09/bronze-age-pervert-costin-alamariu/674762/.

Yost, Julia. "New York's Hottest Club Is the Catholic Church." *New York Times* (August 9, 2022). https://www.nytimes.com/2022/08/09/opinion/nyc-catholicism-dimes-square-religion.html.

Yost, Julia and Matthew Schmitz. "A Conversation between Two Converts." *First Things* (November 12, 2018). https://www.firstthings.com/web-exclusives/2018/11/a-conversation-between-two-converts.

R.J. SNELL is director of academic programs at the Witherspoon Institute in Princeton, NJ, and Editor-in-Chief of *The Public Discourse*. He is the author of many essays in scholarly and popular journals. Recent books include *Mind, Heart, and Soul: Intellectuals and the Path to Rome* (with Robert P. George), and *Acedia and Its Discontents: Metaphysical Boredom in an Empire of Desire.*

Made in United States
Orlando, FL
14 October 2024